20th-CENTURY SCOTTISH POEMS

20th-CENTURY SCOTTISH POEMS

Selected by DOUGLAS DUNN

faber and faber

First published in 2000
by Faber and Faber Limited
3 Queen Square London WC1N 3AU

Photoset by Parker Typesetting Service, Leicester
Printed in Italy

A CIP record for this book
is available from the British Library
ISBN 0–571–20388–4

10 9 8 7 6 5 4 3 2 1

Contents

Preface

Editing *The Faber Book of Twentieth-Century Scottish Poetry* (1992; revised paperback edition, 1993) was an arduous but rewarding task. This book is based on it, but it is not an epitome. Much of the most impressive poetry by Scots has been at length, and a book of this kind precluded spacious representation. It can be read as a sampler. Readers who find what they like here can go to the fuller anthology or to the poets' individual collections. However, I hope the book stands by itself as an anthology of poems worth reprinting and of poets worth recommending for further reading.

Younger poets have been productive since my original selections, and I have changed their inclusions accordingly. Interesting new poets have also appeared since 1993, and I have included a poem by as many as space permitted.

When the original anthology appeared, some reviewers were kind enough to mention that I hadn't included any of my own poems. It was nice to be noticed where I was absent. But an anthologist ought not to include poems which he or she cannot discuss critically. Besides, previous anthologies of Scottish poetry included much by their editors and closest friends, and I hope to be incapable of creating that kind of suspicion. My editorial principles are those of commitment to the subject and disinterestedness. Include me out; or, exclude me in – or whatever Sam Goldwyn's wise howler was.

The term 'twentieth-century' is, of course, an anachronism, or historical. Let it be read as a prelude to 'twenty-first century', and in a spirit that hopes for the perpetuation of good things and an end (as far as possible) to bad.

If there is one point I would like to make it is that the struggles and contests of elder or dead (alas) poets would seem to have been of assistance to the enhanced confidence and relaxation of younger generations of writers.

Douglas Dunn
Dairsie, 20 IX 99

20th-CENTURY SCOTTISH POEMS

VIOLET JACOB (1863–1946)

The Baltic

'Whaur are ye gaen sae fast, my bairn,
  It's no tae the schule ye'll win?'
'Doon tae the shore at the fit o' the toon
  Tae bide till the brigs come in.'

'Awa' noo wi' ye and turn ye hame,
  Ye'll no hae the time tae bide;
It's twa lang months or the brigs come back
  On the lift o' a risin' tide.'

'I'll sit me doon at the water's mou'
  Till there's niver a blink o' licht,
For my feyther bad' me tae tryst wi' him
  In the dairkness o' yesternicht.

'"*Rise ye an' rin tae the shore*", *says he,*
  "*At the cheep o' the waukin' bird,*
And I'll bring ye a tale o' a foreign land
  The like that ye niver heard."'

'Oh, haud yer havers, ye feckless wean,
  It was but a dream ye saw,
For he's far, far north wi' the Baltic men
  I' the hurl o' the Baltic snaw;

And what did he ca' yon foreign land?'
  'He tell'tna its name tae me,
But I doot it's no by the Baltic shore,
  For he said there was nae mair sea.'

blink o' licht, *beam of light*; haud yer havers, *stop your nonsense*; hurl,
violent fall

3

Alas! Poor Queen

She was skilled in music and the dance
And the old arts of love
At the court of the poisoned rose
And the perfumed glove,
And gave her beautiful hand
To the pale Dauphin
A triple crown to win –
And she loved little dogs
    And parrots
  And red-legged partridges
And the golden fishes of the Duc de Guise
And a pigeon with a blue ruff
She had from Monsieur d'Elbœuf.

Master John Knox was no friend to her;
She spoke him soft and kind,
Her honeyed words were Satan's lure
The unwary soul to bind
'Good sir, doth a lissome shape
And a comely face
Offend your God His Grace
Whose Wisdom maketh these
Golden fishes of the Duc de Guise?'

She rode through Liddesdale with a song;
'Ye streams sae wondrous strang,
Oh, mak' me a wrack as I come back
But spare me as I gang,'
While a hill-bird cried and cried
Like a spirit lost
By the grey storm-wind tost.

Consider the way she had to go.
Think of the hungry snare,
The net she herself had woven,
Aware or unaware,
Of the dancing feet grown still,
The blinded eyes –
Queens should be cold and wise,
And she loved little things,
     Parrots
   And red-legged partridges
And the golden fishes of the Duc de Guise
And the pigeon with the blue ruff
She had from Monsieur d'Elbœuf.

LEWIS SPENCE (1874–1955)

The Prows O' Reekie

O wad this braw hie-heapit toun
Sail aff like an enchanted ship,
Drift owre the warld's seas up and doun,
And kiss wi' Venice lip to lip,
Or anchor into Naples' Bay
A misty island far astray
Or set her rock to Athens' wa',
Pillar to pillar, stane to stane,
The cruikit spell o' her backbane,
Yon shadow-mile o' spire and vane,
Wad ding them a', wad ding them a'!
Cadiz wad tine the admiralty
O' yonder emerod fair sea,
Gibraltar frown for frown exchange
Wi' Nigel's crags at elbuck-range,
The rose-red banks o' Lisbon make
Mair room in Tagus for her sake.

A hoose is but a puppet-box
To keep life's images frae knocks,
But mannikins scrieve oot their sauls
Upon its craw-steps and its walls;
Whaur hae they writ them mair sublime
Than on yon gable-ends o' time?

braw, *fine*; ding them a', *surpass them all*; tine, *lose*; emerod, *emerald*;
elbuck, *elbow*; scrieve, *scrape*; craw-steps, *stepped gables*

RACHEL ANNAND TAYLOR (1876–1960)

The Princess of Scotland

'Who are you that so strangely woke,
   And raised a fine hand?'
Poverty wears a scarlet cloke
       In my land.

'Duchies of dreamland, emerald, rose
   Lie at your command?'
Poverty like a princess goes
       In my land.

'Wherefore the mask of silken lace
   Tied with a golden band?'
Poverty walks with wanton grace
       In my land.

'Why do you softly, richly speak
   Rhythm so sweetly-scanned?'
Poverty hath the Gaelic and Greek
       In my land.

'There's a far-off scent about you seems
   Born in Samarkand.'
Poverty hath luxurious dreams
       In my land.

'You have wounds that like passion-flowers you hide:
   I cannot understand.'
Poverty hath one name with Pride
       In my land.

'Oh! Will you draw your last sad breath
   'Mid bitter bent and sand?'
Poverty begs from none but Death
       In my land.

On the Pilgrims' Road

That I had hit the Road
   I partly knew
From a great Roman snail
   And sombre yew;
But that my steps went from
   And not towards
The shrine of good St Thomas,
   I thought of afterwards.

So I adored today
   No, not his ghost,
But the saints in Westwell window,
   And her the most
Who knelt there with no head
   But was so very
Adorable a saint
   In dress of crushed strawberry.

The Shepherd's Hut

The smear of blue peat smoke
That staggered on the wind and broke,
The only sign of life,
Where was the shepherd's wife,
Who left those flapping clothes to dry,
Taking no thought for her family?
For, as they bellied out
And limbs took shape and waved about,
I thought, She little knows
That ghosts are trying on her children's clothes.

EDWIN MUIR (1887–1959)

The Horses

Barely a twelvemonth after
The seven days war that put the world to sleep,
Late in the evening the strange horses came.
By then we had made our covenant with silence,
But in the first few days it was so still
We listened to our breathing and were afraid.
On the second day
The radios failed; we turned the knobs; no answer.
On the third day a warship passed us, heading north,
Dead bodies piled on the deck. On the sixth day
A plane plunged over us into the sea. Thereafter
Nothing. The radios dumb;
And still they stand in corners of our kitchens,
And stand, perhaps, turned on, in a million rooms
All over the world. But now if they should speak,
If on a sudden they should speak again,
If on the stroke of noon a voice should speak,
We would not listen, we would not let it bring
That old bad world that swallowed its children quick
At one great gulp. We would not have it again.
Sometimes we think of the nations lying asleep,
Curled blindly in impenetrable sorrow,
And then the thought confounds us with its strangeness.

The tractors lie about our fields; at evening
They look like dank sea-monsters couched and waiting.
We leave them where they are and let them rust:
'They'll moulder away and be like other loam'.
We make our oxen drag our rusty ploughs,
Long laid aside. We have gone back
Far past our fathers' land.
                              And then, that evening

Late in the summer the strange horses came.
We heard a distant tapping on the road,
A deepening drumming; it stopped, went on again
And at the corner changed to hollow thunder.
We saw the heads
Like a wild wave charging and were afraid.
We had sold our horses in our fathers' time
To buy new tractors. Now they were strange to us
As fabulous steeds set on an ancient shield
Or illustrations in a book of knights.
We did not dare go near them. Yet they waited,
Stubborn and shy, as if they had been sent
By an old command to find our whereabouts
And that long-lost archaic companionship.
In the first moment we had never a thought
That they were creatures to be owned and used.
Among them were some half-a-dozen colts
Dropped in some wilderness of the broken world,
Yet new as if they had come from their own Eden.
Since then they have pulled our ploughs and borne our loads
But that free servitude still can pierce our hearts.
Our life is changed; their coming our beginning.

HUGH MACDIARMID (Christopher Murray Grieve)
(1892–1978)

The Bonnie Broukit Bairn
For Peggy

Mars is braw in crammasy,
Venus in a green silk goun,
The auld mune shak's her gowden feathers,
Their starry talk's a wheen o' blethers,
Nane for thee a thochtie sparin',
Earth, thou bonnie broukit bairn!
– *But greet, an' in your tears ye'll droun*
The haill clanjamfrie!

braw in crammasy, *fine in crimson*; wheen o' blethers, *bit of nonsense*;
broukit bairn, *neglected child*; greet, *weep*; the haill clanjamfrie, *the whole
of worthless humanity*

The Watergaw

Ae weet forenicht i' the yow-trummle
I saw yon antrin thing,
A watergaw wi' its chitterin' licht
Ayont the on-ding;
An' I thocht o' the last wild look ye gied
Afore ye deed!

There was nae reek i' the laverock's hoose
That nicht – an' nane i' mine;
But I hae thocht o' that foolish licht
Ever sin' syne;

An' I think that mebbe at last I ken
What your look meant then.

watergaw, *broken rainbow*; weet forenicht, *wet dusk*; yow-trummle, *ewe-tremble (a cold spell in summer after sheep-shearing)*; antrin, *rare*; ayont the on-ding, *beyond the downpour*; reek, *quarrel*; laverock, *lark*; sin' syne, *since then*

The Eemis Stane

I' the how-dumb-deid o' the cauld hairst nicht
The warl' like an eemis stane
Wags i' the lift;
An' my eerie memories fa'
Like a yowdendrift.

Like a yowdendrift so's I couldna read
The words cut oot i' the stane
Had the fug o' fame
An' history's hazelraw
No' yirdit thaim.

eemis, *unsteady*; how-dumb-deid, *at the very heart*; hairst, *harvest*; i' the lift, *in the sky*; yowdendrift, *snow blown in the air*; fug, *moss*; hazelraw, *lichen*; yirdit, *buried*

O Wha's the Bride?
(*from* A Drunk Man Looks at the Thistle)

O wha's the bride that cairries the bunch
O' thistles blinterin' white?
Her cuckold bridegroom little dreids
What he sall ken this nicht.

For closer than gudeman can come
And closer to'r than hersel',

Wha didna need her maidenheid
Has wrocht his purpose fell.

O wha's been here afore me, lass,
And hoo did he get in?
    – *A man that deed or I was born*
    This evil thing has din.

And left, as it were on a corpse
Your maidenheid to me?
    – *Nae lass, gudeman, sin' Time began*
    'S hed ony mair to gi'e.

But I can gi'e ye kindness, lad,
And a pair o' willin' hands,
And you sall ha'e my briests like stars,
My limbs like willow wands,

And on my lips ye'll heed nae mair,
And in my hair forget,
The seed o' a' the men that in
My virgin womb ha'e met . . .

blinterin, *glimmering*; dreids, *suspects*; gudeman, *husband*

WILLIAM SOUTAR (1898–1943)

The Tryst

O luely, luely cam she in
And luely she lay doun:
I kent her by her caller lips
And her breists sae sma' and roun'.

A' thru the nicht we spak nae word
Nor sinder'd bane frae bane:
A' thru the nicht I heard her hert
Gang soundin' wi' my ain.

It was about the waukrife hour
Whan cocks begin to craw
That she smool'd saftly thru the mirk
Afore the day wud daw.

Sae luely, luely, cam she in
Sae luely was she gaen
And wi' her a' my simmer days
Like they had never been.

luely, *softly*; caller, *cool*; sinder'd bane frae bane, *parted bone from bone*;
waukrife, *wakeful*; smool'd saftly, *slipped away*

14

NORMAN CAMERON (1905–53)

Green, Green is El Aghir

Sprawled on the crates and sacks in the rear of the truck,
I was gummy-mouthed from the sun and the dust of the
    track.
And the two Arab soldiers I'd taken on as hitch-hikers
At a torrid petrol-dump, had been there on their hunkers
Since early morning. I said, in a kind of French
'On m'a dit, qu'il y a une belle source d'eau fraîche.
Plus loin, à El Aghir' . . .

                    It was eighty more kilometres
Until round a corner we heard a splashing of waters,
And there, in a green, dark street, was a fountain with two
    faces
Discharging both ways, from full-throated faucets
Into basins, thence into troughs and thence into brooks.
Our negro corporal driver slammed his brakes,
And we yelped and leapt from the truck and went at the
    double
To fill our bidons and bottles and drink and dabble.
Then, swollen with water, we went to an inn for wine.
The Arabs came, too, though their faith might have stood
    between.
'After all,' they said, 'it's a boisson,' without contrition.

Green, green is El Aghir. It has a railway-station,
And the wealth of its soil has borne many another fruit,
A mairie, a school and an elegant Salle de Fêtes.
Such blessings, as I remarked, in effect, to the waiter,
Are added unto them that have plenty of water.

ROBERT GARIOCH (Robert Garioch Sutherland)
(1909–81)

Glisk of the Great

I saw him comin out the N.B. Grill,
creashy and winey, wi his famous voice
crackin some comic bawr to please three choice
notorious bailies, lauchan fit to kill.

Syne thae fowre crousie cronies clam intill
a muckle big municipal Rolls-Royce,
and disappeared, aye lauchan, wi a noise
that droont the traffic, towards the Calton Hill.

As they rade by, it seemed the sun was shinin
brichter nor usual roun thae cantie three
that wi thon weill-kent Heid-yin had been dinin.

Nou that's the kinna thing I like to see;
tho ye and I look on and canna jyne in,
it gies our toun some tone, ye'll aa agree.

glisk, *glimpse*; creashy, *greasy*; bawr, *joke*; bailies, *magistrates*; lauchan,
laughing; crousie, *merry*; clam, *climbed*; muckle big, *great big*; cantie,
cheerful; weill-kent Heid-yin, *well-known magnifico*

Heard in the Cougate

'Whu's aa thae fflagpoles ffur in Princes Street?
Chwoich! Ptt! Hechyuch! Ab-boannie cairry-on.
Seez-owre the wa'er. Whu' the deevil's thon
inaidie, heh?' 'The Queen's t'meet

The King o Norway wi his royal suite.'
'His royal wh'?' 'The hale jing-bang. It's aw in
the papur. Whaur's ma speck-sh? Aye they're gaun
t'day-cor-ate the toun. It's a fair treat,

something ye dinnae see jist ivry day,
foun'uns in the Gairdens, muckle spates
dancing t'music, an thir's t'be nae

chairge t'gi'in, it aw gaes on the Rates.'
'Ah ddae-ken whu' the pplace is comin tae
wi aw thae, hechyuch! fforeign po'entates.'

Summer Farm

Straws like tame lightnings lie about the grass
And hang zigzag on hedges. Green as glass
The water in the horse-trough shines.
Nine ducks go wobbling by in two straight lines.

A hen stares at nothing with one eye,
Then picks it up. Out of an empty sky
A swallow falls and, flickering through
The barn, dives up again into the dizzy blue.

I lie, not thinking, in the cool, soft grass,
Afraid of where a thought might take me – as
This grasshopper with plated face
Unfolds his legs and finds himself in space.

Self under self, a pile of selves I stand
Threaded on time, and with metaphysic hand
Lift the farm like a lid and see
Farm within farm, and in the centre, me.

Byre

The thatched roof rings like heaven where mice
Squeak small hosannahs all night long,
Scratching its golden pavements, skirting
The gutter's crystal river-song.

Wild kittens in the world below
Glare with one flaming eye through cracks,
Spurt in the straw, are tawny brooches
Splayed on the chests of drunken sacks.

The dimness becomes darkness as
Vast presences come mincing in,
Swagbellied Aphrodites, swinging
A silver slaver from each chin.

And all is milky, secret, female.
Angels are hushed and plain straws shine.
And kittens miaow in circles, stalking
With tail and hindleg one straight line.

Old Edinburgh

Down the Canongate
down the Cowgate
go vermilion dreams
snake's tongues of bannerets
trumpets with words from their mouths
saying *Praise me, praise me.*

Up the Cowgate
up the Canongate
lice on the march
tar on the amputated stump
Hell speaking with the tongue of Heaven
a woman tied to the tail of a cart.

And history leans by a dark entry
with words from his mouth
that say *Pity me, pity me*
but never forgive.

SORLEY MACLEAN (Somhairle Macgill-Eain) (1911–96)

Glac a' Bhàis

Thubhairt Nàsach air choireigin gun tug am Furair air ais do fhir na Gearmailte 'a' chòir agus an sonas bàs fhaotainn anns an àraich'

'Na shuidhe marbh an 'Glaic a' Bhàis'
fo Dhruim Ruidhìseit,
gill' òg 's a logan sìos m' a ghruaidh
's a thuar grìsionn.

Smaoinich mi air a' chòir's an àgh
a fhuair e bho Fhurair,
bhith tuiteam ann an raon an àir
gun éirigh tuilleadh;

air a' ghreadhnachas's air a' chliù
nach d' fhuair e 'na aonar,
ged b' esan bu bhrònaiche snuadh
ann an glaic air laomadh

le cuileagan mu chuirp ghlas'
air gainmhich lachduinn
's i salach-bhuidhe 's làn de raip
's de sprùidhlich catha.

An robh an gille air an dream
a mhàb na h-Iùdhaich
's na Comunnaich, no air an dream
bu mhotha, dhiùbh-san

a threòraicheadh bho thoiseach àl
gun deòin gu buaireadh
agus bruaillean cuthaich gach blàir
air sgàth uachdaran?

Ge b'e a dheòin-san no a chàs,
a neoichiontas no mhìorun,
cha do nochd e toileachadh 'na bhàs
fo Dhruim Ruidhìseit.

Death Valley

*Some Nazi or other has said that the Fuehrer had restored to
German manhood the 'right and joy of dying in battle'*

Sitting dead in 'Death Valley'
below the Ruweisat Ridge
a boy with his forelock down about his cheek
and his face slate-grey;

I thought of the right and the joy
that he got from his Fuehrer,
of falling in the field of slaughter
to rise no more;

of the pomp and the fame
that he had, not alone,
though he was the most piteous to see
in a valley gone to seed

with flies about grey corpses
on a dun sand
dirty yellow and full of the rubbish
and fragments of battle.

Was the boy of the band
who abused the Jews
and Communists, or of the greater
band of those

led, from the beginning of generations,
unwillingly to the trial
and mad delirium of every war
for the sake of rulers?

Whatever his desire or mishap,
his innocence or malignity,
he showed no pleasure in his death
below the Ruweisat Ridge.

Hallaig

'Tha tìm, am fiadh, an coille Hallaig'

Tha bùird is tàirnean air an uinneig
troimh 'm faca mi an Aird an Iar
's tha mo ghaol aig Allt Hallaig
'na craoibh bheithe, 's bha i riamh

eadar an t-Inbhir 's Poll a' Bhainne,
thall 's a bhos mu Bhaile-Chùirn:
tha i 'na beithe, 'na calltuinn,
'na caorunn dhìreach sheang ùir.

Ann an Screapadal mo chinnidh,
far robh Tarmad 's Eachunn Mór,
tha 'n nigheanan 's am mic 'nan coille
ag gabhail suas ri taobh an lóin.

Uaibhreach a nochd na coilich ghiuthais
ag gairm air mullach Cnoc an Rà,
dìreach an druim ris a' ghealaich –
chan iadsan coille mo ghràidh.

Fuirichidh mi ris a' bheithe
gus an tig i mach an Càrn,
gus am bi am bearradh uile
o Bheinn na Lice f' a sgàil.

Mura tig 's ann theàrnas mi a Hallaig
a dh'ionnsaigh sàbaid nam marbh,
far a bheil an sluagh a' tathaich,
gach aon ghinealach a dh' fhalbh.

Tha iad fhathast ann a Hallaig,
Clann Ghill-Eain's Clann MhicLeòid,
na bh' ann ri linn Mhic Ghille-Chaluim:
Chunnacas na mairbh beò.

Na fir 'nan laighe air an lianaig
aig ceann gach taighe a bh' ann,
na h-igheanan 'nan coille bheithe,
direach an druim, crom an ceann.

Eadar an Leac is na Feàrnaibh
tha 'n rathad mór fo chóinnich chiùin,
's na h-igheanan 'nam badan sàmhach
s' dol a Chlachan mar o thùs.

Agus a' tilleadh as a' Chlachan,
á Suidhisnis 's á tir nam beò;
a chuile té òg uallach
gun bhristeadh cridhe an sgeòil.

O Allt na Feàrnaibh gus an fhaoilinn
tha soilleir an dìomhaireachd nam beann
chan eil ach coimhthional nan nighean
ag cumail na coiseachd gun cheann.

A' tilleadh a Hallaig anns an fheasgar,
anns a' chamhanaich bhalbh bheò,
a' lìonadh nan leathadan casa,
an gàireachdaich 'nam chluais 'na ceò,

's am bòidhche 'na sgleò air mo chridhe
mun tig an ciaradh air na caoil,
's nuair theàrnas grian air cùl Dhùn Cana
thig peileir dian á gunna Ghaoil;

's buailear am fiadh a tha 'na thuaineal
a' snòtach nan làraichean feòir;
thig reothadh air a shùil 'sa' choille:
chan fhaighear lorg air fhuil ri m' bheò.

Hallaig

'Time, the deer, is in the wood of Hallaig'

The window is nailed and boarded
through which I saw the West
and my love is at the Burn of Hallaig,
a birch tree, and she has always been

between Inver and Milk Hollow,
here and there about Baile-chuirn:
she is a birch, a hazel,
a straight, slender young rowan.

In Screapadal of my people
where Norman and Big Hector were,
their daughters and their sons are a wood
going up beside the stream.

Proud tonight the pine cocks
crowing on the top of Cnoc an Ra,
straight their backs in the moonlight –
they are not the wood I love.

I will wait for the birch wood
until it comes up by the cairn,
until the whole ridge from Beinn na Lice
will be under its shade.

If it does not, I will go down to Hallaig,
to the Sabbath of the dead,
where the people are frequenting,
every single generation gone.

They are still in Hallaig,
MacLeans and MacLeods,
all who were there in the time of Mac Gille Chaluim
the dead have been seen alive.

The men lying on the green
at the end of every house that was,
the girls a wood of birches,
straight their backs, bent their heads.

Between the Leac and Fearns
the road is under mild moss
and the girls in silent bands
go to Clachan as in the beginning,

and return from Clachan,
from Suisnish and the land of the living;
each one young and light-stepping,
without the heartbreak of the tale.

From the Burn of Fearns to the raised beach
that is clear in the mystery of the hills,
there is only the congregation of the girls
keeping up the endless walk,

coming back to Hallaig in the evening,
in the dumb living twilight,
filling the steep slopes,
their laughter a mist in my ears,

and their beauty a film on my heart
before the dimness comes on the kyles,
and when the sun goes down behind Dun Cana
a vehement bullet will come from the gun of Love;

and will strike the deer that goes dizzily,
sniffing at the grass-grown ruined homes;
his eye will freeze in the wood,
his blood will not be traced while I live.

A Burial

Of one who was much to me,
Nothing to anyone else,
I shall have least to say,
For silence is not false.
Once when I walked in iron
Through dead formalities,
I wished that I need not summon
The barbarous preaching voice.
So simple an act as death
Needs no pomp to excuse,
Nor any expense of breath
To magnify what is.
The sun shot the red apples,
Flies swung on summer air,
The world swam in green ripples
As a slow sea might stir.
There is no more to do
But to turn and go away,
Turn and finally go
From one who was much to me,
Nothing to anyone else.
Often it must be so
And always words be false.
Child, do you blame what is?
Child, do you blame what was?

DOUGLAS YOUNG (1913–73)

For a Wife in Jizzen

Lassie, can ye say
    whaur ye ha been,
whaur ye ha come frae,
    whatna ferlies seen?

Eftir the bluid and swyte,
    the warsslin o yestreen,
ye ligg forfochten, whyte,
    prouder nor onie Queen.

Albeid ye hardly see me
    I read it i your een,
sae saft blue and dreamy,
    mindan whaur ye've been.

Anerly wives ken
    the ruits of joy and tene,
        the march o daith and birth,
            the tryst o love and strife
i the howedumbdeidsuinsheen,
        fire, air, water, yirth
            mellan to mak new life,
lauchan and greetan, feiman and serene.

Dern frae aa men
    the ferlies ye ha seen.

jizzen, *childbed*; ferlies, *marvels*; warsslin, *struggling*; forfochten,
exhausted; nor, *than*; albeid, *although*; mindan, *remembering*; anerly,
only; tene, *grief*; howedumbdeidsuinsheen, *midnight sunshine*; mellan,
mixing; lauchan, *laughing*; greetan, *weeping*; feiman, *passionate*; dern,
hide

RUTHVEN TODD (1914–1978)

Trout Flies
for J.K.M.

Ten years of age and intent upon a tea-brown burn
Across a moor in Lanarkshire, brass reel and greenheart
Rod, my first, I tried them out and came to learn
These magic names, from which I now can never part.

The insignificant ones were best, so ran the story
Of the old man who slowly taught me how to cast:
Dark Snipe, perhaps, Cow Dung, or favourite Greenwell's
   Glory,
Would attract the sleek trout that moved so fast

To attack and suck the right and only fly.
Gaudy Partridge & Orange could be used, he said,
By those who fished on lochs, *his* fish would shy
From bright Butcher, Cardinal, or Teal & Red.

Now, on a clear day, a Wickham's Fancy might
Deceive a hungry trout, or even a Red Spinner,
But Coch-y-Bondu, or March Brown, in failing light,
Were more certain to bring home the dinner.

Watching the dull fly settle gently on the water
I would await the tug and make my strike,
While these names became a permanent mortar
Between my memories, names that I like

And tongue familiarly, Black Midge and August Dun,
Blue Upright, Cinnamon Sedge, Coachman and Pheasant
   Tail,
Red Ant, Red Hackle, Furnace Palmer, and Yellow Sally, in
   the sun,
Ghost, Green Midge, Half Stone and, sometimes, Never Fail.

G. S. FRASER (1914–80)

Home Town Elegy
For Aberdeen in Spring

Glitter of mica at the windy corners,
Tar in the nostrils, under blue lamps budding
Like bubbles of glass the blue buds of a tree,
Night-shining shopfronts, or the sleek sun flooding
The broad abundant dying sprawl of the Dee:
For these and for their like my thoughts are mourners
That yet shall stand, though I come home no more,
Gas-works, white ballroom, and the red brick baths
And salmon nets along a mile of shore,
Or beyond the municipal golf-course, the moorland paths
And the country lying quiet and full of farms.
This is the shape of a land that outlasts a strategy
And is not to be taken with rhetoric or arms.
Or my own room, with a dozen books on the bed
(Too late, still musing what I mused, I lie
And read too lovingly what I have read),
Brantôme, Spinoza, Yeats, the bawdy and wise,
Continuing their interminable debate,
With no conclusion, they conclude too late,
When their wisdom has fallen like a grey pall on my eyes.
Syne we maun part, their sall be nane remeid –
Unless my country is my pride, indeed,
Or I can make my town that homely fame
That Byron has, from boys in Carden Place,
Struggling home with books to midday dinner,
For whom he is not the romantic sinner,
The careless writer, the tormented face,

The hectoring bully or the noble fool,
But, just like Gordon or like Keith, a name:
A tall, proud statue at the Grammar School.

SYDNEY GOODSIR SMITH (1915–75)

Slugabed (*from* Under the Eildon Tree)

Here I ligg, Sydney Slugabed Godless Smith,
The Smith, the Faber, ποιητής and Makar,
And Oblomov has nocht to learn me,
Auld Oblomov has nocht on me
Liggan my lane in bed at nune
Gantan at gray December haar,
A cauld, scummie, hauf-drunk cup o' tea
    At my bed-side,
    Luntan Virginian fags
– The New World thus I haud in fief
And levie kyndlie tribute. Black men slave
Aneath a distant sun to mak for me
Cheroots at hauf-a-croun the box.
  Wi ase on the sheets, ase on the cod,
And crumbs of toast under my bum,
Scrievan the last great coronach
O' the westren flickeran bourgeois world.
  Eheu fugaces!
                  Lacrimæ rerum!
Nil nisi et cætera ex cathedra
                  Requiescat up your jumper.

 O, michtie Stalin in the Aist!
Could ye but see me nou,
The type, endpynt and final blume
O' decadent capitalistical thirldom
  – It took five hunder year to produce me –
Och, could ye but see me nou
What a sermon could ye gie
  Further frae the Hailie Kremlin
Bummlan and thunderan owre the Steppes,

Athort the mountains o' Europe humman
Till Swack! at my front door, the great *Schloss Schmidt*
That's *Numéro Cinquante* (ПЯТЬДЕСЯТ* ye ken)
In the umquhile pairk o' Craigmillar House
Whar Marie Stewart o the snawie blee
Aince plantit ane o' a thousand treen.
  Losh, what a sermon yon wad be!
For Knox has nocht on Uncle Joe
And Oblomov has nocht on Smith
  And sae we come by a route maist devious
  Til the far-famed Aist-West Synthesis!
  Beluved by Hugh that's beluved by me
And the baith o' us loe the barley-bree –
But wha can afford to drink the stuff?
  Certies no auld Oblomov!
  – And yet he does! Whiles!
But no as muckle as Uncle Joe – I've smaa dout!
НА ЗГОРОВЬЕ* then, auld Muscovite!

Thus are the michtie faaen,
Thus the end o' a michtie line,
Dunbar til Smith the Slugabed
Whas luve burns brichter nor them aa
And whas dounfaain is nae less,
  Deid for a ducat deid
By the crueltie o' his ain maistress.

ligg, *lie*; my lane, *alone*; gantan, *gaping*; haar, *mist*; ase, *ash*; cod, *pillow*;
coronach, *elegy*; thirldom, *servitude*; bummlan, *bustling*; humman,
humming; umquhile, *former*; blee, *complexion*; loe, *love*; barley-bree,
whisky; no as muckle, *not as much*; dounfaain, *downfall*

* piat' desiat, *fifty*; Na zdrorovye, *good health*

GEORGE CAMPBELL HAY (Deorsa Caimbeul Hay)
(1915–84)

Bisearta

Chi mi rè geàrd na h-oidhche
dreòs air chrith 'na fhroidhneas thall air fàire,
a' clapail le a sgiathaibh,
a' sgapadh 's a' ciaradh rionnagan na h-àird' ud.

Shaoileadh tu gun cluinnte,
ge cian, o 'bhuillsgein ochanaich no caoineadh,
ràn corruich no gàir fuatha,
comhart chon cuthaich uaidh no ulfhairt fhaolchon,
gun ruigeadh drannd an fhòirneirt
o'n fhùirneis òmair iomall fhéin an t-saoghail;
ach sud a' dol an leud e
ri oir an speur an tosdachd olc is aognaidh.

C' ainm nochd a th' orra,
na sràidean bochda anns an sgeith gach uinneag
a lasraichean 's a deatach,
a sradagan is sgreadail a luchd thuinidh,
is taigh air thaigh 'ga reubadh
am broinn a chéile am brùchdadh toit a' tuiteam?
Is có an nochd tha 'g atach
am Bàs a theachd gu grad 'nan cainntibh uile,
no a' spàirn measg chlach is shailthean
air bhàinidh a' gairm air cobhair, is nach cluinnear?
Cò an nochd a phàidheas
sean chìs àbhaisteach na fala cumant?

Uair dearg mar lod na h-àraich,
uair bàn mar ghile thràighte an eagail éitigh,
a' dìreadh 's uair a' teàrnadh,
a' sìneadh le sitheadh àrd 's a' call a mheudachd,

33

a' fannachadh car aitil
's ag at mar anail dhiabhail air dhéinead,
an t-Olc 'na chridhe 's 'na chuisle,
chì mi 'na bhuillean a' sìoladh 's a' leum e.
Tha 'n dreòs 'na oillt air fàire,
'na fhàinne ròis is òir am bun nan speuran,
a' breugnachadh 's ag àicheadh
le shoillse sèimhe àrsaidh àrd nan reultan.

Bizerta

I see during the night guard
a blaze flickering, fringing the skyline over yonder,
beating with its wings
and scattering and dimming the stars of that airt.

You would think that there would be heard
from its midst, though far away, wailing and lamentation,
the roar of rage and the yell of hate,
the barking of the dogs from it or the howling of wolves,
that the snarl of violence would reach
from yon amber furnace the very edge of the world;
but yonder it spreads
along the rim of the sky in evil ghastly silence.

What is their name tonight,
the poor streets where every window spews
its flame and smoke,
its sparks and the screaming of its inmates,
while house upon house is rent
and collapses in a gust of smoke?
And who tonight are beseeching
Death to come quickly in all their tongues,
or are struggling among stones and beams,
crying in frenzy for help, and are not heard?

Who tonight is paying
the old accustomed tax of common blood?

Now red like a battlefield puddle,
now pale like the drained whiteness of foul fear,
climbing and sinking,
reaching and darting up and shrinking in size,
growing faint for a moment
and swelling like the breath of a devil in intensity,
I see Evil as a pulse
and a heart declining and leaping in throbs.
The blaze, a horror on the skyline,
a ring of rose and gold at the foot of the sky,
belies and denies
with its light the ancient high tranquillity of the stars.

The Lying Dear

At entrance cried out but not
For me (Should I have needed it?)
Her bitching eyes under
My pressing down shoulder
Looked up to meet the face
In cracks on the flaking ceiling
Descending. The map of damp
Behind me, up, formed
Itself to catch the look
Under the closed (now)
Lids of my lying dear.

Under my pinning arm
I suddenly saw between
The acting flutters, a look
Catch on some image not me.

With a hand across her eyes
I changed my weight of all
Knowledge of her before.
And like a belly sledge
I steered us on the run
Mounting the curves to almost
The high verge. Her breath
Flew out like smoke. Her beauty
Twisted into another
Beauty and we went down
Into the little village
Of a new language.

The Stepping Stones

I have my yellow boots on to walk
Across the shires where I hide
Away from my true people and all
I can't put easily into my life.

So you will see I am stepping on
The stones between the runnels getting
Nowhere nowhere. It is almost
Embarrassing to be alive alone.

Take my hand and pull me over from
The last stone on to the moss and
The three celandines. Now my dear
Let us go home across the shires.

TOM SCOTT (1918–95)

The Mankind Toun
For Shirley Bridges

Hou lang we've socht
I dinna ken
For a toun that micht
Be fit for men.
Ten thousant year
Or mair or less
But yond or here
Wi smaa success.

We've fled mirk Thebes
Wi Ikhnaton,
Fleggit the grebes
By Babylon
And sat in quorum,
Man til man
In Karakorum
Wi Jenghis Khan.

Seen Nineveh,
Byzantium,
Sidon, Troy,
Cartaga, Rome;
Corinth, wi its
Wreathit touers,
Damascan streets
Wi Asterte's whures;
Been amang the tents
Round Samarkan
And alang the bents
By Trebizon.

Frae Nippur, Tyre,
Jerusalem,
Athens, Palmyra,
Pergamum
Til Florence, Venice,
The toun on Thames,
Imperial Vienna's
Waltzan dames,
Braw touns we've seen,
And will again,
But nane that hes been
Fit for men.

Shall we never find
The toun whaur love
Rules mankind?
Whaur the hawk, the dove,
And houlet form
A trinitie
That keeps frae hairm
Ilk chimney tree?
Whaur first is laist
And ilk and ane
Gie free their best
Til brither-men?

Whiles it seems
It canna be,
Binna in dreams;
Or till we see
The minarets,
The spires that rise
Abuin the yetts
O paradise.

But na, we'll find
Midnicht or noon,
Our vaigin's end,
The mankind toun:
Yet bidan true
Til the Sender's aims
Seek further new
Jerusalems.

fleggit, *startled*; bents, *bent-grass*; houlet, *owl*; ilk, *each*; binna, *unless*;
abuin the yetts, *above the gates*; vaigin, *journey*

MURIEL SPARK (b. 1918)

Elegy in a Kensington Churchyard

Lady who lies beneath this stone,
Pupil of Time pragmatical,
Though in a lifetime's cultivation
You did not blossom, summer shall.

The fierce activity of grass
Assaults a century's constraint.
Vigour survives the vigorous,
Meek as you were, or proud as paint.

And bares its fist for insurrection
Clenched in the bud; lady who lies
Those leaves will spend in disaffection
Your fond estate and purposes.

Death's a contagion: spring's a bright
Green fit; the blight will overcome
The plague that overcame the blight
That laid this lady low and dumb,

And laid a parish on its back
So soon amazed, so long enticed
Into an earthy almanack,
And musters now the spring attack;
Which render passive, latent Christ.

Seven Good Germans (Seventh Elegy)

The track running between Mekili and Tmimi was at one time a
kind of no-man's-land. British patrolling was energetic, and there
were numerous brushes with German and Italian elements. El Eleba
lies about half-way along this track.

Of the swaddies
who came to the desert with Rommel
there were few who had heard (or would hear) of El Eleba.

They recce'd,
        or acted as medical orderlies
or patched up their tanks in the camouflaged workshops
and never gave a thought to a place like El Eleba.

To get there, you drive into the blue, take a bearing
and head for damn-all. Then you're there. And where are
    you?

– Still, of some few who did cross our path at El Eleba
there are seven who bide under their standing crosses.

The first a Lieutenant.
        When the medicos passed him
for service overseas, he had jotted in a note-book
to the day and the hour   keep me steadfast   there
is only the decision and the will
                the rest has no importance

The second a Corporal.
                He had been in the Legion
and had got one more chance to redeem his lost honour.

What he said was
Listen here, I'm fed up with your griping –
If you want extra rations, go get 'em from Tommy!
You're green, that's your trouble. Dodge the column, pass the
  buck
and scrounge all you can – that's our law in the Legion.
You know Tommy's got 'em. . . . He's got mineral waters,
and beer, and fresh fruit in that white crinkly paper
and God knows what all! Well, what's holding you back?
Are you windy or what?
                    Christ, you 'old Afrikaners'!
If you're wanting the eats, go and get 'em from Tommy!

The third had been a farm-hand in the March of Silesia
and had come to the desert as fresh fodder for machine guns.
His dates are inscribed on the files, and on the cross-piece.

The fourth was a lance-jack.
                    He had trusted in Adolf
while working as a chemist in the suburb of Spandau.
His loves were his 'cello, and the woman who had borne him
two daughters and a son. He had faith in the Endsieg.
THAT THE NEW REICH MAY LIVE prayed the flyleaf of his
  Bible.

The fifth a mechanic.
                    All the honour and glory,
the siege of Tobruk and the conquest of Cairo
meant as much to that Boche as the Synod of Whitby.
Being wise to all this, he had one single headache,
which was, how to get back to his sweetheart (called Ilse).
– He had said
          Can't the Tommy wake up and get weaving?
If he tried, he could put our whole Corps in the bag.
May God damn this Libya and both of its palm-trees!

The sixth was a Pole

         – or to you, a Volksdeutscher –

who had put off his nation to serve in the Wehrmacht.
He siegheiled, and talked of 'the dirty Polacken,'
and said what he'd do if let loose among Russkis.
His mates thought that, though 'just a polnischer
    Schweinhund',
he was not a bad bloke.

                 On the morning concerned
he was driving a truck with mail, petrol and rations.
The MP on duty shouted five words of warning.
He nodded

       laughed

             revved

                   and drove straight for El Eleba
not having quite got the chap's Styrian lingo.

The seventh a young swaddy.

                Riding cramped in a lorry
to death along the road which winds eastward to Halfaya
he had written three verses in appeal against his sentence
which soften for an hour the anger of Lenin.

                Seven poor bastards
                dead in African deadland
                (tawny tousled hair under the issue blanket)
                wie einst Lili
                dead in African deadland
                     einst Lili Marlene

ALEXANDER SCOTT (1920–89)

Coronach
For the dead of the 5/7th Battalion, The Gordon Highlanders

Waement the deid
I never did,
Owre gled I was ane o the lave
That somewey baid alive
To trauchle my thowless hert
Wi ithers' hurt.

But nou that I'm far
Frae the fechtin's fear,
Nou I hae won awa frae aa thon pain
Back til my beuks and my pen,
They croud aroun me out o the grave
Whaur love and langourie sae lanesome grieve.

Cryan the cauld words:
'We hae dree'd our weirds,
But you that byde ahin,
Ayont our awesome hyne,
You are the flesh we aince had been,
We that are bruckle brokken bane.'

Cryan a drumlie speak:
'You hae the words we spak,
You hae the sang
We canna sing,
Sen death maun skail
The makar's skill.

'Makar, frae nou ye maun
Be singan for us deid men,
Sing til the warld we loo'd
(For aa that its brichtness lee'd)
And tell hou the sudden nicht
Cam doun and made us nocht.'

Waement the deid
I never did,
But nou I am safe awa
I hear their wae
Greetan greetan dark and daw,
Their death the-streen my darg the-day.

coronach, *lament*; waement, *lament*; ane o the lave, *one of the remainder*;
baid, *stayed*; trauchle, *trouble*; thowless, *spiritless*; fechtin, *fighting*; beuks,
books; langourie, *longing*; dree'd our weirds, *endured our fates*; byde ahin,
remain behind; ayont, *beyond*; hyne, *haven*; bruckle, *brittle*; brokken,
broken; drumlie speak, *dull speech*; maun skail, *must disperse*; makar,
poet; loo'd, *loved*; lee'd, *lied*; nocht, *nothing*; greetan, *weeping*; daw, *dawn*;
the-streen, *yesterday*; darg, *work*

Cinquevalli

Cinquevalli is falling, falling.
The shining trapeze kicks and flirts free,
solo performer at last.
The sawdust puffs up with a thump,
settles on a tangle of broken limbs.
St Petersburg screams and leans.
His pulse flickers with the gas-jets. He lives.

Cinquevalli has a therapy.
In his hospital bed, in his hospital chair
he holds a ball, lightly, lets it roll round his hand,
or grips it tight, gauging its weight and resistance,
begins to balance it, to feel its life attached to his
by will and knowledge, invisible strings
that only he can see. He throws it
from hand to hand, always different,
always the same, always
different, always the
same.
His muscles learn to think, his arms grow very strong.

Cinquevalli in sepia
looks at me from an old postcard: bundle of enigmas.
Half faun, half military man; almond eyes, curly hair,
conventional moustache; tights, and a tunic loaded
with embroideries, tassels, chains, fringes; hand on hip
with a large signet-ring winking at the camera
but a bull neck and shoulders and a cannon-ball
at his elbow as he stands by the posing pedestal;
half reluctant, half truculent,
half handsome, half absurd,
but let me see you forget him: not to be done.

Cinquevalli is a juggler.
In a thousand theatres, in every continent,
he is the best, the greatest. After eight years perfecting
he can balance one billiard ball on another billiard ball
on top of a cue on top of a third billiard ball
in a wine-glass held in his mouth. To those
who say the balls are waxed, or flattened,
he patiently explains the trick will only work
because the spheres are absolutely true.
There is no deception in him. He is true.

Cinquevalli is juggling with a bowler,
a walking-stick, a cigar, and a coin.
Who foresees? How to please.
The last time round, the bowler
flies to his head, the stick sticks in his hand,
the cigar jumps into his mouth, the coin
lands on his foot – ah, but
is kicked into his eye
and held there as the miraculous monocle
without which the portrait would be incomplete.

Cinquevalli is practising.
He sits in his dressing-room talking to some friends,
at the same time writing a letter with one hand
and with the other juggling four balls.
His friends think of demons, but
'You could do all this,' he says,
sealing the letter with a billiard ball.

Cinquevalli is on the high wire in Odessa.
The roof cracks, he is falling, falling
into the audience, a woman breaks his fall,
he cracks her like a flea, but lives.

Cinquevalli broods in his armchair in Brixton Road.
He reads in the paper about the shells whining
at Passchendaele, imagines the mud and the dead.
He goes to the window and wonders through that dark
     evening
what is happening in Poland where he was born.
His neighbours call him a German spy.
'Kestner, Paul Kestner, that's his name!'
'Keep Kestner out of the British music-hall!'
He frowns; it is cold; his fingers seem stiff and old.

Cinquevalli tosses up a plate of soup
and twirls it on his forefinger; not a drop spills.
He laughs, and well may he laugh
who can do that. The astonished table
breathe again, laugh too, think the world
a spinning thing that spills, for a moment, no drop.

Cinquevalli's coffin sways through Brixton
only a few months before the Armistice.
Like some trick they cannot get off the ground
it seems to burden the shuffling bearers, all their arms
cross-juggle that displaced person, that man
of balance, of strength, of delights and marvels,
in his unsteady box at last into the earth.

The Coin

We brushed the dirt off, held it to the light.
The obverse showed us *Scotland*, and the head
of a red deer; the antler-glint had fled
but the fine cut could still be felt. All right:
we turned it over, read easily *One Pound*,
but then the shock of Latin, like a gloss,
Respublica Scotorum, sent across
such ages as we guessed but never found

at the worn edge where once the date had been
and where as many fingers had gripped hard
as hopes their silent race had lost or gained.
The marshy scurf crept up to our machine,
sucked at our boots. Yet nothing seemed ill-starred.
And least of all the realm the coin contained.

The First Men on Mercury

– We come in peace from the third planet.
Would you take us to your leader?

– Bawr stretter! Bawr. Bawr. Stretterhawl?

– This is a little plastic model
of the solar system, with working parts.
You are here and we are there and we
are now here with you, is this clear?

– Gawl horrop. Bawr. Abawrhannahanna!

– Where we come from is blue and white
with brown, you see we call the brown
here 'land', the blue is 'sea', and the white
is 'clouds' over land and sea, we live
on the surface of the brown land
all round is sea and clouds. We are 'men'.
Men come –

– Glawp men! Gawrbenner menko. Menhawl?

– Men come in peace from the third planet
which we call 'earth'. We are earthmen.
Take us earthmen to your leader.

– Thmen? Thmen? Bawr. Bawrhossop.
Yuleeda tan hanna. Harrabost yuleeda.

– I am the yuleeda. You see my hands,
we carry no benner, we come in peace.
The spaceways are all stretterhawn.

– Glawn peacemen all horrabhanna tantko!
Tan come at'mstrossop. Glawp yuleeda!

– Atoms are peacegawl in our harraban.
Menbat worrabost from tan hannahanna.

– You men we know bawrhossoptant. Bawr.
We know yuleeda. Go strawg backspetter quick.

– We cantantabawr, tantingko backspetter now!

– Banghapper now! Yes, third planet back.
Yuleeda will go back blue, white, brown
nowhanna! There is no more talk.

– Gawl han fasthapper?

– No. You must go back to your planet.
Go back in peace, take what you have gained
but quickly.

– Stretterworra gawl, gawl . . .

– Of course, but nothing is ever the same,
now is it? You'll remember Mercury.

DERICK THOMSON (Ruaraidh MacThomais)
(b. 1921)

An Tobar

Tha tobar beag am meadhon a' bhaile
's am feur ga fhalach,
am feur gorm sùghor ga dhlùth thughadh,
fhuair mi brath air bho sheann chaillich,
ach thuirt i, 'Tha 'm frith-rathad fo raineach
far am minig a choisich mi le'm chogan,
's tha'n cogan fhèin air dèabhadh.'
Nuair sheall mi 'na h-aodann preasach
chunnaic mi 'n raineach a' fàs mu thobar a sùilean
's ga fhalach bho shireadh 's bho rùintean,
's ga dhùnadh 's ga dhùnadh.

'Cha teid duine an diugh don tobar tha sin'
thuirt a' chailleach, 'mar a chaidh sinne
nuair a bha sinn òg,
ged tha 'm bùrn ann cho brèagh 's cho geal.'
'S nuair sheall mi troimhn raineach 'na sùilean
chunnaic mi lainnir a' bhùirn ud
a ni slàn gach ciùrradh
gu ruig ciùrradh cridhe.

'Is feuch an tadhail thu dhòmhsa,'
thuirt a' chailleach, 'ga b'ann le meòirean,
's thoir thugam boinne den uisge chruaidh sin
a bheir rudhadh gu m' ghruaidhean.'
Lorg mi an tobar air èiginn
's ged nach b'ise bu mhotha feum air
'sann thuice a thug mi 'n eudail.

Dh' fhaodadh nach eil anns an tobar
ach nì a chunnaic mi 'm bruadar,
oir nuair chaidh mi an diugh ga shireadh
cha d'fhuair mi ach raineach is luachair,
's tha sùilean na caillich dùinte
's tha lì air tighinn air an luathghair.

The Well

Right in the village there's a little well
and the grass hides it,
green grass in sap closely thatching it.
I heard of it from an old woman
but she said: 'The path is overgrown with bracken
where I often walked with my cogie,
and the cogie itself is warped.'
When I looked in her lined face
I saw the bracken growing round the well of her eyes,
and hiding it from seeking and from desires,
and closing it, closing it.

'Nobody goes to that well now,'
said the old woman, 'as we once went,
when we were young,
though its water is lovely and white.'
And when I looked in her eyes through the bracken
I saw the sparkle of that water
that makes whole every hurt
till the hurt of the heart.

'And will you go there for me,'
said the old woman, 'even with a thimble,
and bring me a drop of that hard water

that will bring colour to my cheeks.'
I found the well at last,
and though her need was not the greatest
it was to her I brought the treasure.

It may be that the well
is something I saw in a dream,
for today when I went to seek it
I found only bracken and rushes,
and the old woman's eyes are closed
and a film has come over their merriment.

Srath Nabhair

Anns an adhar dhubh-ghorm ud,
àirde na sìorraidheachd os ar cionn,
bha rionnag a' priobadh ruinn
's i freagairt mireadh an teine
ann an cabair taigh m' athar
a' bhlianna thugh sinn an taigh le bleideagan sneachda.

Agus siud a' bhlianna cuideachd
a shlaod iad a' chailleach don t-sitig,
a shealltainn cho eòlach 's a bha iad air an Fhìrinn,
oir bha nid aig eunlaith an adhair
(agus cròthan aig na caoraich)
ged nach robh àit aice-se anns an cuireadh i a ceann fòidhpe.

A Shrath Nabhair 's a Shrath Chill Donnain,
is beag an t-iongnadh ged a chinneadh am fraoch àlainn
    oirbh,
a' falach nan lotan a dh' fhàg Pàdraig Sellar 's a sheòrsa,
mar a chunnaic mi uair is uair boireannach cràbhaidh
a dh' fhiosraich dòrainn an t-saoghail-sa
is sìth Dhè 'na sùilean.

Strathnaver

In that blue-black sky,
as high above us as eternity,
a star was winking at us,
answering the leaping flames of fire
in the rafters of my father's house,
that year we thatched the house with snowflakes.

And that too was the year
they hauled the old woman out on to the dung-heap,
to demonstrate how knowledgeable they were in Scripture,
for the birds of the air had nests
(and the sheep had folds)
though she had no place in which to lay down her head.

O Strathnaver and Strath of Kildonan,
it is little wonder that the heather should bloom on your slopes,
hiding the wounds that Patrick Sellar, and such as he, made,
just as time and time again I have seen a pious woman
who has suffered the sorrow of this world,
with the peace of God shining from her eyes.

Old Fisherman with Guitar

A formal exercise for withered fingers.
  The head is bent,
    The eyes half closed, the tune
Lingers
    And beats, a gentle wing the west had thrown
    Against his breakwater wall with salt savage lament.

So fierce and sweet the song on the plucked string,
  Know now for truth
    Those hands have cut from the net
The strong
    Crag-eaten corpse of Jock washed from a boat
    One old winter, and gathered the mouth of Thora to his
mouth.

Trout Fisher

Semphill, his hat stuck full of hooks
  Sits drinking ale
    Among the English fishing visitors,
  Probes in detail
    Their faults in casting, reeling, selection of flies.
'Never,' he urges, 'do what it says in the books'.
    Then they, obscurely wise,
    Abandon by the loch their dripping oars
    And hang their throttled tarnish on the scale.

'Forgive me, every speckled trout',
　　Says Semphill then,
　　　　'And every swan and eider on these waters.
　　Certain strange men
　　　　Taking advantage of my poverty
Have wheedled all my subtle loch-craft out
　　　　So that their butchery
　　　　Seem fine technique in the ear of wives and daughters.
　　And I betray the loch for a white coin.'

Kirkyard

A silent conquering army,
The island dead,
Column on column, each with a stone banner
Raised over his head.

A green wave full of fish
Drifted far
In wavering westering ebb-drawn shoals beyond
Sinker or star.

A labyrinth of celled
And waxen pain.
Yet I come to the honeycomb often, to sip the finished
Fragrance of men.

WILLIAM NEILL (b. 1922)

Map Makers

When Irongray grew out of *Earran Reidh*
the culture could not stand on level ground.
Grey dominies of unmalleable will
invented newer legends of their own
to satisfy the blacksmith and his children.

After *Cill Osbran* closed up to Closeburn
more books were shut than Osbran's psalter.
Seeking to baptize the new born name
the pedants hurried to the nearest water
which wasn't even warm.

When *Seann Bhaile* swelled to Shambelly
the old steading became a glutton's belch.
Every tourist pointed a magic finger
padding lean Fingal to a flabby Falstaff.

The cold men in the city
who circumscribe all latitude
wiped their bullseye glasses
laid down the stabbing pens
that had dealt the mortal wounds
slaying the history of a thousand years
in the hour between lunch and catching the evening train.

dominies, *schoolmasters*

IVOR CUTLER (b. 1923)

The Railway Sleepers

The railway sleepers
heavy and dry
from old workingwomen's bones.

Trains press over like stout husbands.

Jacket vest and trousers
smelling of cloth and husband
lay black on a chair
not responding to light.

My nose on the pillow.
Breath flows along the cotton hollows.

A bare bulb
yellow in the signal box.

The heavy sleepers lie dark.
Creak under the frost.

A starving bush
perched on the verge
shrieks at dense air out the tunnel
tearing its twigs.
Ends of roots
suck cinders for organic compounds.

The signalman
is noticing his painted tea-flask
on the sill.
He picks his nose without knowing.
Snot drops about his feet.

Dawn
gleams like mercury
afraid to come up.

ALASTAIR REID (b. 1926)

Scotland

It was a day peculiar to this piece of the planet,
when larks rose on long thin strings of singing
and the air shifted with the shimmer of actual angels.
Greenness entered the body. The grasses
shivered with presences, and sunlight
stayed like a halo on hair and heather and hills.
Walking into town, I saw, in a radiant raincoat,
the woman from the fish-shop. 'What a day it is!'
cried I, like a sunstruck madman.
And what did she have to say for it?
Her brow grew bleak, her ancestors raged in their graves
as she spoke with their ancient misery:
'We'll pay for it, we'll pay for it, we'll pay for it!'

IAIN CRICHTON SMITH (1928–98)

The Law and the Grace

It's law they ask of me and not grace.
'Conform,' they say, 'your works are not enough.
Be what we say you should be,' even if
graceful hypocrisy obscures my face.

'We know no angels. If you say you do
that's blasphemy and devilry.' Yet I have
known some bright angels, of spontaneous love.
Should I deny them, be to falsehood true,

the squeeze of law which has invented torture
to bring the grace to a malignant head?
Do you want me, angels, to be wholly dead?
Do you need, black devils, steadfastly to cure

life of itself? And you to stand beside
the stone you set on me? No, I have angels. Mine
are free and perfect. They have no design
on anyone else, but only on my pride,

my insufficiency, imperfect works.
They often leave me but they sometimes come
to judge me to the core, till I am dumb.
Is this not law enough, you patriarchs?

Chinese Poem

1

To Seumas Macdonald,
                          now resident in Edinburgh –
I am alone here, sacked from the Department
for alcoholic practices and disrespect.
A cold wind blows from Ben Cruachan.
There is nothing here but sheep and large boulders.
Do you remember the nights with *Reliquae Celticae*
and those odd translations by Calder?
Buzzards rest on the wires. There are many seagulls.
My trousers grow used to the dung.
What news from the frontier? Is Donald still Colonel?
Are there more pupils than teachers in Scotland?
I send you this by a small boy with a pointed head.
Don't trust him. He is a Campbell.

2

The dog brought your letter today
from the red postbox on the stone gate
two miles away and a bit.
I read it carefully with tears in my eyes.
At night the moon is high over Cladach
and the big mansions of prosperous Englishmen.
I drank a half bottle thinking of Meg
and the involved affairs of Scotland.
When shall we two meet again
in thunder, lightning or in rain?
The carrots and turnips are healthy,
the *Farmers' Weekly* garrulous.
Please send me a *Radio Times* and a book
on cracking codes. I have much sorrow.
Mrs Macleod has a blue lion on her pants.
They make a queenly swish in a high wind.

3

There is a man here who has been building a house
for twenty years and a day.
He has a barrow in which he carries large stones.
He wears a canvas jacket.
I think I am going out of my mind.
When shall I see the city again,
its high towers and insurance offices,
its glare of unprincipled glass?
The hens peck at the grain.
The wind brings me pictures of exiles,
ghosts in tackety boots, lies,
adulteries in cornfields and draughty cottages.
I hear Donald is a brigadier now
and that there is fighting on the frontier.
The newspapers arrive late with strange signs on them.
I go out and watch the road.

4

Today I read five books.
I watched Macleod weaving a fence
to keep the eagles from his potatoes.
A dull horse is cobwebbed in rain.
When shall our land consider itself safe
from the assurance of the third rate mind?
We lack I think nervous intelligence.
Tell them I shall serve in any capacity,
a field officer, even a private,
so long as I can see the future
through uncracked field glasses.

5

A woman arrived today
in a brown coat and a brown muff.
She says we are losing the war,
that the Emperor's troops are everywhere
in their blue armour and blue gloves.
She says there are men in a stupor
in the ditches among the marigolds
crying 'Alas, alas.'
I refuse to believe her.
She is, I think, an agent provocateur.
She pretends to breed thistles.

Listen

Listen, I have flown through darkness towards joy,
I have put the mossy stones away from me,
and the thorns, the thistles, the brambles.
I have swum upward like a fish

through the black wet earth, the ancient roots
which insanely fight with each other
in a grave which creates a treasure house
of light upward-springing leaves.

Such joy, such joy! Such airy drama
the clouds compose in the heavens,
such interchange of comedies,
disguises, rhymes, denouements.

I had not believed that the stony heads
would change to actors and actresses,
and that the grooved armour of statues
would rise and walk away

into a resurrection of villages,
townspeople, citizens, dead exiles,
who sing with the salt in their mouths,
winged nightingales of brine.

Peterhead in May

Small lights pirouette
Among these brisk little boats.
A beam, cool as a butler,
Steps from the lighthouse.

Wheelroom windows are dark.
Reflections of light quickly
Skip over them tipsily like
A girl in silk.

One knows there is new paint
And somehow an intense
Suggestion of ornament
Comes into mind.

Imagine elephants here.
They'd settle, clumsily sure
of themselves and of us and of four
Square meals and of water.

Then you will have it. This
Though a grey and quiet place
Finds nothing much amiss.
It keeps its stillness.

There is no wind. A thin
Mist fumbles above it and,
Doing its best to be gone,
Obscures the position.

This place is quiet or,
Better, impersonal. There
Now you have it. No verdict
Is asked for, no answer.

Yet nets will lie all morning,
Limp like stage scenery,
Unused but significant
Of something to come.

GEORGE MACBETH (1932–92)

Draft for an Ancestor

When I was young, and wrote about him first,
My Uncle Hugh was easier to hold.
      Now, in my age, at worst
    I take him by some outer fold
Of what was his. His Humber, by the door.
    That, at the least, if nothing more

Creates an image of his prosperous time
And thumbs in waistcoats to suggest their power.
      I hear tall glasses chime
    And clocks from walnut sound the hour
As they drive to Derby, where their horse will lose.
    At last, it seems, men have to choose

What traits in relatives they will to raise
To the height of models, awkward, fey, or strong,
      And there arrange as praise
    For the unhooked soul, keen to belong
To its family, some tree of love and grace
    In which there blossoms no mean face.

I feel this drive. As years go by, it grows
And I want an ancestry of heroic mould
      Fit for a world that knows
    How to accept the subtly bold
Who grasp at shields and leaves with a sprig of wit
    And honours their effrontery with it.

So Uncle Hugh, that self-made, stubborn man
I see in photographs, and hear in my head,
      Provides a flash of élan
    To the ranks of my more sombre dead
And, startling, floods their quarters with his brash
      And flighty Scottish kind of dash.

CHRISTOPHER SALVESEN (b. 1935)

History of Strathclyde

How earth was made, I might have had it sung,
How life began – hushed rocking of the tide
Lapping the sleepy margins of the world.

But – searching back into almost unsearchable
Time (and yet, the waters have always stirred) –
Footprints tell a different order of fact:
Three-toed, Batrachian, printed in the rocks,
In the flaggy sandstone of Euchan Water
In the upper reaches of Nithsdale – early
Exploratory steps as the moment passed;
Petrified, along with suncracks and ripples,
Like those of any casual hen or dog
On a wet concrete path – the same sun shone.

Ah but the earth, this grassy land, has changed.
These pitted marks I long to think are raindrops
More properly interpreted as sea-spray:
No fossil bones or plants remain to help us
But – carcasses and all organic debris
Devoured by scavengers and scouring tides –
It was a coast, the glaring salty shore
Where bushy banks run now and the rowans sway.

A kingdom in the history of man,
A Dark Age kingdom and in that well named –
So little known of family and fighting,
Thus easily guessed at but so hard to grasp –
It was a border, and a middle ground,
As the power of Rome withdrew: other tides,
Less tied to the moon's control, carried on
The moves of life, washed over them as well.

Today in the bright afternoon I saw,
As I walked a drove-road towards the north,
The black-faced ewes cropping the heathery hills,
One, by the track, seeming asleep: except –
A neat dark-red pit in the bony face –
The crows had pecked its eyes out: for a moment,
As the sun went on with its mindless work,
In that wool hulk, a history of Strathclyde.

KENNETH WHITE (b. 1936)

from Late August on the Coast

A SHORT INTRODUCTION TO WHITE POETICS

Consider first the Canada Goose
brown body, whitish breast
black head, long black neck
with a white patch from throat to cheek
bill and legs black
flies in regular chevron or line formation
flight note: *aa-honk*
(that's the one old Walt heard on Long Island)

Then there's the Barnacle Goose
black and white plumage
white face and forehead
(in German, it's *Weisswangengans*)
flight in close ragged packs
flight note
a rapidly repeated *gnuk:*
gnuk gnuk gnuk gnuk gnuk gnuk gnuk
(like an ecstatic Eskimo)

Look now at the Brent Goose
small and dark
black head, neck and breast
brilliant white arse
more sea-going than other geese
feeds along the coast
by day or by night
rapid flight
seldom in formation

irregularly changing flocks
her cry:
a soft, throaty gut-bucket *rronk*

The Red-Breasted Goose
has a combination of
black, white and chestnut plumage
legs and bill blackish
quick and agile, this beauty
seldom flies in regular formation
cry:
a shrill *kee-kwa kee-kwa*
(who, what? who, what?)

The Greylag
pale grey forewings
thick orange bill
lives near the coastline
flies to grazing grounds at dawn
usually in regular formation
cry: *aahng ung-ung*
(like a Chinese poet
exiled in Mongolia)

As to the Bean Goose
she has a dark forewing
and a long black bill
talks a lot less than other geese
just a low, rich, laconic *ung-unk*

The Snow Goose
has a pure white plumage
with blacktipped wings
dark pink bill and legs
(in North America turns blue
a dusky blue-grey)
in Europe you might take her for a swan
or maybe a gannet

till she lets you know abruptly
with one harsh *kaank*
she's all goose

so
there they go
through the wind, the rain, the snow

wild spirits
knowing what they know

Todd

My father's white uncle became
    Arthritic and testamental in
    Lyrical stages. He held cardinal sin
Was misuse of horses, then any game

Won on the sabbath. A Clydesdale
    To him was not bells and sugar or declension
    From paddock, but primal extension
Of rock and soil. Thundered nail

Turned to sacred bolt. And each night
    In the stable he would slaver and slave
    At cracked hooves, or else save
Bowls of porridge for just the right

Beast. I remember I lied
    To him once, about oats: then I felt
    The brand of his loving tongue, the belt
Of his own horsey breath. But he died,

When the mechanised tractor came to pass.
    Now I think of him neighing to some saint
    In a simple heaven or, beyond complaint,
Leaning across a fence and munching grass.

On Craigie Hill

The farmhouse seems centuries ago,
The steadings slouched under a sifting of snow
For weeks on end, lamps hissing, logs stacked
Like drums in the shed, the ice having to be cracked
To let the shaggy cats drink. Or
Back from the mart through steaming pastures
Men would come riding – their best
Boots gleaming, rough tweeds pressed
To a knife-edge, pockets stuffed with notes.

Before that even, I could visualise (from coloured
Prints) traps rattling, wheels spinning; furred
Figures posing like sepia dolls
In a waxen world of weddings and funerals.
When Todd died, last of the old-stagers,
Friends of seventy years followed the hearse.
Soon the farm went out of the family; the Cochranes
Going to earth or, like their cousins,
Deciding it was time to hit town.

The last link broken, the farm-buildings stand
In a clutter below the quarry. The land
Retains its richness – but in other hands.
Kilmarnock has encroached. It is hard to look
Back with any sense of belonging.
Too much has changed, is still changing.
This blustery afternoon on Craigie Hill
I regard remotely the muddy track
My father used to trudge along, to school.

ROBIN FULTON (b. 1937)

Resolutions

All day the air got harder and harder.
I woke in the small hours, rooftops

frozen seas of tranquillity, while far
below the first flakes fell on the street.

The air of another planet come down to earth,
we breathe harshly between familiar stones.

No place for flesh. Spirit and bone
at odds, the nerves caught between, singing:

'Must it be?' It must be must be must be
bouncing like a ball in a small room without windows.

D. M. BLACK (b. 1941)

Kew Gardens

In memory of Ian A. Black, died January 1971

Distinguished scientist, to whom I greatly defer
(old man, moreover, whom I dearly love),
I walk today in Kew Gardens, in sunlight the colour of honey
which flows from the cold autumnal blue of the heavens to
    light these tans and golds,
these ripe corn and leather and sunset colours of the East
    Asian liriodendrons,
of the beeches and maples and plum-trees and the stubborn
    green banks of the holly hedges –
and you walk always beside me, you with your knowledge of
    names
and your clairvoyant gaze, in what for me is sheer panorama
seeing the net or web of connectedness. But today it is I who
    speak
(and you are long dead, but it is to you I say it):

'The leaves are green in summer because of chlorophyll
and the flowers are bright to lure the pollinators,
and without remainder (so you have often told me)
these marvellous things that shock the heart the head can
    account for;
but I want to sing an excess which is not so simply
    explainable,
to say that the beauty of the autumn is a redundant beauty,
that the sky had no need to be this particular shade of blue,
nor the maple to die in flames of this particular yellow,
nor the heart to respond with an ecstasy that does not beget
    children.
I want to say that I do not believe your science

although I believe every word of it, and intend to understand
    it
that although I rate that unwavering gaze higher than almost
    everything
there is another sense, a hearing, to which I more deeply
    attend.
Thus I withstand and contradict you, I, your child,
who have inherited from you the passion which causes me to
    oppose you.'

from an cathadh mor

3

mìorbhail an t-sneachda
gach criostal àraid
gach criostal gun chàraid
meanbh-chlachaireachd
gach lóineag a' tàthadh
saoghal fo chidhis

sneachda fìorghlan
    (ìocshlaint nan galair
    fras chalman air iteal
    mealltach mesmearach)
sneachda gun lochd
    (cléireach ag ùrnaigh
    an cille stàilinn
    ghlas a chreideimh
    cléireach a' guidhe
    fhradharc 'na bhoisean
    ag àicheadh a bhruadar)

sneachda lainnireach
    (leanabh a' ruidhleadh aig uinneig
    sùilean a' dealradh)
sneachda grioglannach
    (speuran brùite   dùinte)
sneachda brìodalach
    snàigeach sniagach
sneachda lìonmhorachadh
    sàmhach sàmhach

sneachda càrnach
sneachda fillteach
sneachda casgrach

6

sìneadh a h-éididh air
cathair   caisteal   clachan

sgaoileadh a còt' air
gach buaile   gach bealach
gach sgurr is gach rubha
h-uile sràid anns gach baile
geal   geal   geal

plangaid air saoghal
brat-sìth do threubhan domhain

an gilead gealltanach   gluasadach

8

chan fhaic an t-iasgair ach cobhar
sgorran is sgeirean fo chobhar
sgaothan a' gluasad

                        thar a' chala
                        thar an raoin
                        thar an t-sléibh
cha dhearc a shùil air cuan air cala
chan fhaic e ach cobhar nan sgaoth
a' traoghadh air raointean

an eathar 'na taibhse air teadhair
a lìn nan greasain gheal bhreòiteach
oillsginn gun anam a' crochadh is
      bòtainnean laighe mar chuirp

sluaghan a' chuain do-ruigsinn

from *the great snowbattle*

3

marvel of snow
every crystal unique
every crystal without peer
micro-masonry
every flake cementing
a world beneath its mask

virginal snow
         (balm for plagues
         flurry of flying doves
         deceptive, deadening)
faultless snow
         (a cleric prays
         in the steel cell
         of his credo
         cleric beseeches,
         his sight in his palms
         denying his dreams)

brilliant snow
         (child dancing at window
         eyes reflect glitter)
constellated snow
         (the skies are bruised   enclosed)
cajoling snow
         snaking sneaking
multiplying snow
         silent silent
mounding snow
pleating snow
slaughtering snow

6

stretching her raiment on
city   castle   clachan

spreading her coat on
each meadow   each pass
each peak and each reef
all the streets in each town
white   white   white

a blanket on the world
a flag of truce for
all the tribes in a universe

the whiteness promising   shifting

8

the fisher sees nothing but foam
summits and skerries are under the spray
shoals are moving
                    over harbours
                    across fields
                    across the moors
his eye cannot see ocean, anchorage
he sees only foaming shoals
subsiding on meadows

the boat is a tethered ghost
his nets white friable webs
his oilskins hang soulless while
    boots are outstretched corpses

ocean's multitudes are out of reach

ALAN BOLD (1943–98)

A Special Theory of Relativity

According to Einstein
There's no still centre of the universe:
Everything is moving
Relative to something else.
My love, I move myself towards you,
Measure my motion
In relation to yours.

According to Einstein
The mass of a moving body
Exceeds its mass
When standing still.
My love, in moving
Through you
I feel my mass increase.

According to Einstein
The length of a moving body
Diminishes
As speed increases.
My love, after accelerating
Inside you
I spectacularly shrink.

According to Einstein
Time slows down
As we approach
The speed of light.
My love, as we approach
The speed of light
Time is standing still.

ALISON FELL (b. 1944)

Pushing Forty

Just before winter
we see the trees show
their true colours:
the mad yellow of chestnuts
two maples like blood sisters
the orange beech
braver than lipstick

Pushing forty, we vow
that when the time comes
rather than wither
ladylike and white
we will henna our hair
like Colette, we too
will be gold and red
and go out
in a last wild blaze

IAN ABBOT (1944–89)

A Body of Work

Do you not see, finally,
how the earth is moving to inhabit me?

My teeth
are the white stones of the river-bed;
throughout the day
an otter dozes in the dank holt of my mouth.
The sinews of my legs
go down into the earth like roots, and knots of shifting clay
compose the muscles of my face.
My hair, my sex becoming
clumps of hoary winter grass.

Seasons are manifest in me:
I know their white, their green, their turning yellow.
Laughing, my voice is the fever of stags; the pure
transparency of leaves is in my speech. Constellations
sift their burning atoms through my veins.

But in singing, weeping,
waking in the night and crying out,
my language is a deer dismembered under pines,
bloody and netted with shadows.
An intricate labyrinth of entrails,
lit from within
and patiently transfigured to the lightning grin of bones.

TOM LEONARD (b. 1944)

from Unrelated Incidents

1

its thi lang-
wij a thi
guhtr thaht hi
said its thi
langwij a
thi guhtr

awright fur
funny stuff
ur
Stanley Bax-
ter ur but
luv n science
n thaht naw

thi langwij
a thi
intillect hi
said thi lang-
wij a thi intill-
ects Inglish

then whin thi
doors slid
oapn hi raised
his hat geen
mi a fare-
well nod flung
oot his right

fit boldly n
fell eight
storeys
doon thi
empty
lift-shaft

from Ghostie Men

right inuff
ma language is disgraceful

ma maw tellt mi
ma teacher tellt mi
thi doactir tellt mi
thi priest tellt mi

ma boss tellt mi
ma landlady in carrington street tellt mi
thi lassie ah tried tay get aff way in 1969 tellt mi
sum wee smout thit thoat ah hudny read chomsky tellt mi
a calvinistic communist thit thoat ah wuz revisionist tellt mi

po-faced literati grimly kerryin thi burden a thi past tellt mi
po-faced literati grimly kerryin thi burden a thi future tellt
   mi
ma wife tellt mi jist-tay-get-inty-this-poem tellt mi
ma wainz came hame fray school an tellt mi
jist aboot ivry book ah oapnd tellt mi
even thi introduction tay thi Scottish National Dictionary
   tellt mi

ach well
all livin language is sacred
fuck thi lohta thim

LIZ LOCHHEAD (b. 1947)

The Grim Sisters

And for special things
(weddings, school-
concerts) the grown up girls next door
would do my hair.

Luxembourg announced *Amami Night*.

I sat at peace passing bobbipins
from a marshmallow pink cosmetic purse
embossed with jazzmen,
girls with pony tails and a November
topaz lucky birthstone.
They doused my cow's-lick, rollered
and skewered tightly.
I expected that to be lovely
would be worth the hurt.

They read my Stars,
tied chiffon scarves to doorhandles, tried
to teach me tight dancesteps
you'd no guarantee
any partner you might find would ever be able to
keep up with as far as I could see.

There were always things to burn
before the men came in.

For each disaster
you were meant to know the handy hint.
Soap at a pinch
but better nailvarnish (clear) for ladders.
For kisscurls, spit.

Those days womanhood was quite a sticky thing
and that was what these grim sisters came to mean.

'You'll know all about it soon enough.'
But when the clock struck they
stood still, stopped dead.
And they were left there
out in the cold with the wrong skirtlength
and bouffant hair,
dressed to kill,

who'd been
all the rage in fifty-eight,
a swish of Persianelle
a slosh of perfume.
In those big black mantrap handbags
they snapped shut at any hint of *that*
were hedgehog hairbrushes
cottonwool mice and barbed combs to tease.
Their heels spiked bubblegum, dead leaves.

Wasp waist and cone breast, I see them yet.
I hope, I hope
there's been a change of more than silhouette.

My Mother's Suitors

have come to court me
have come to call oh
yes with their wonderful world
war two moustaches their long
stem roses their cultivated
accents (they're English aren't they
at very least they're
educated-Scots).
They are absolutely
au fait with menu-French

they know the language of flowers
& oh they'd die
rather than send a dozen yellow
they always get them right & red.
Their handwriting on the florist's card
slants neither too much to the left or right.

They are good sorts.
They have the profile for it – note
the not too much nose
the plenty chin. The
stockings they bring have no strings
& their square
capable hands are forever
lifting your hair and gently
pushing your head away from them
to fumble endearingly at your nape
with the clasp of the pretty heirloom
little necklace they know their
grandmother would have wanted
you to have.
(Never opals – they know
that pearls mean tears).

They have come to call & we'll all
go walking under the black sky's
droning big bombers
among the ratatat of ack-ack.
We'll go dancing & tonight
shall I wear the lilac, or the
scarlet, or the white?

VALERIE GILLIES (b. 1948)

The Ericstane Brooch

The gold cross-bow brooch,
The Emperors' gift to an officer,
Was lost on the upland moor.
The pierced work and the inscription
Lay far from human habitation.

It worked on time and space
And they were at work on it.
What could withstand them?
But it was waiting for the human,
To address itself to a man or woman.

In the wilderness it meant nothing.
The great spaces dissolved its image,
Time obliterated its meaning.
Without being brought in,
It was less than the simplest safety-pin.

Now the brooch is transporting the past
To the present, the far to the near.
Between the two, its maker and wearer
And watcher live mysteriously.
Who is this who values it so seriously?

It exists, it has been seen by him.
If it speaks, it can only say
'He lost me.' And we reply, 'Who?
For he can also be our loss,
This moment floating face-down in the moss.'

Dumb replica: the original is in Los Angeles.
How is it, the man once destroyed,
His brooch continues boundlessly?
Our very existence is what it defies:
We no longer see what once we scrutinized.

RON BUTLIN (b. 1949)

This Evening

You placed yellow roses by the window, then,
leaning forwards, began combing your red hair;
perhaps you were crying.
To make the distance less I turned away
and faced you across the earth's circumference.

The window-pane turns black:
across its flawed glass suddenly your image
runs on mine.
I stare at the vase until yellow
is no longer a colour, nor the roses flowers.

TOM POW (b. 1950)

from The Gift of Sight

SAINT MEDAN

That Medan was beautiful,
    there was no doubt.
Wherever she went,
    hearts were routed.

But, to her, these looks
    were but a costume
she couldn't cast off.
    She saw her fortune

not in the fancy
    of romantic play –
it was in inner things
    her interests lay.

Medan took a vow
    of chastity; her life
she bound to Christ.
    It was a sharp knife

in the hearts of men.
    But one noble knight
did not believe her.
    To quit his sight

she left Ireland
    for green Galloway.
To the Rhinns she came,
    to live in poverty.

The knight followed.
    He would die or wed
his heart's crusade.
    Pure Medan now fled

to a rock in the sea.
    With prayer, the rock
became a boat;
    the boat she took

thirty miles away.
    Still, he followed;
blindly obeying
    what the hollow

in his heart called for.
    He'd have been lost,
but a crowing cock –
    to both their costs –

told him the house
    where Medan lay.
Shaken, she climbed
    and she prayed

as she climbed
    into a thorn tree.
From there, she asked,
    'What do you see

in me to excite
    your passion?' 'Your face
and eyes,' he replied.
    She sighed, 'In which case . . .'

then impaled her eyes
    on two sharp thorns
and flung them at him.
    Desire was torn

forever from that knight.
    He looked at his feet,
where the eyes had rolled –
    lustrous jade, now meat

for ants. Horror-struck,
    he left – a penitent.
Medan washed her face,
    for a spring – heaven-sent –

gurgled from the dry earth.
    The rest of her days
were lived in poverty
    and sanctity. (*Praise*

the Lord, sang Ninian.)
    The proud cock half-lived,
but crowed no more.
    And sight became the gift

Saint Medan gave,
    so that all could suffer
in equal measure,
    beauty and terror.

Slug

Don't you fancy me in my black
figure-hugging bodystocking
skin?

Watch me arch my agile back,
show my underside's pale line –
like an inky, questing tongue.

Do I disgust you?
I am not the only libido
to ooze from this dark earth.

Haven't we met somewhere
before? What are you doing here
on this rainy afternoon, alone?

My tapering finger is beckoning
you to your likeness.
Come on.

GERALD MANGAN (b. 1951)

Heraclitus at Glasgow Cross

Where Gallowgate meets London Road
    and the world walks out with his wife,
umbrellas sail in long flotillas
    through streets you can't cross twice.

The old home town looks just the same
    when you step down off the Sixty-Three.
The jukebox music takes you back
    to the green, green grass of Polmadie.

Everything swarms and eddies in smirr.
    Wine flows out from the Saracen's Head.
Mascara runs, like soot from a guttering.
    Day-glo signs glow green on red.

Something for Everyone. Nothing for Nothing.
    Social Security Estimates Free.
It's Scotland's Friendliest Market-Place.
    Watch Your Handbags, Ladies, Please.

Watch the Do-nuts fry in grease,
    the tailgate-auctioneers compete
with the broken-winded squeezebox player,
    wheezing through his leaking pleats.

Or under Clyde Street's railway arches,
    see the stubbled dossers soak
like debris snagged in shallows, blowing
    old Virginia up in smoke.

Down where the fishwives trade in rags,
    they curl like snails in paper shells:
lips of sponge, skins of mould,
    eyes like cinders doused in hell.

They're watching concrete fill the docks,
  the bollards rust on the graving-quays.
The green green grass grows overhead,
  on gantries still as gallows-trees.

Where Gorbals faces Broomielaw,
  the river's black and still as ice.
When the ferryman takes the fare, he says
  You can cross this river twice.

smirr, *drizzle*

In the Tool-shed

'Hummingbirds' he said, and spat. Winged tongues
hovered in the half-light of their names;
cat, cobra, cockatoo rose hissing from the juice.
Piece-time in Africa, amid the terrapins
and jerrycans! Steam swirled above the Congo
of his cup, mangrove-rooted fingers plugged the air –
'Baboons? Make sure you look them in the eyes.' Birds
of paradise! Parrots, paraffin, parakeets
flashed blue and raucous through
thickets of swoe, scythe, riddle, adze.
He sat bow-backed and slack in the dark
heart of his kingdom – creator, guide
in that jungle of sounds, boxes, cloches, canes,
twine, twill, galoshes, jumbled all
across, over, through and into one another
from floor to roof, prowled by fabled carnivores,
the jaguar! the secateurs! Words poke
wet muzzles through reeds of sound
grown enormous overnight. Twin depths
of pitch and pitcher! Elephants lean
patiently upon their ponderous names.
They come in clutches: azaleas, zebras, zambesi.
Orchids, oranges, oran-utangs hang
from their common mouth. Lemming, gorilla, lynx
slink nose to tail through mango groves,
drenched in this sibilant monsoon: moonstone, machetes,
peacocks, paw-paws, lepers, leopards – the walls
are creaking but hold them all, swaying, sweating,
in that dark continent between the ears.
Easy, easy genesis! Old witchdoctor, gardener,
deity of the shed, I grew that garden

from his words, caught the fever
pitch of his Niagara; I follow still
the Orinoco of his blue forearm veins
that beat among the talking drums
of all my childhood afternoons.

from Passing Through Doorways (Part I)

i

I can no longer remain in this building,
Not after this latest turn of events;
After I have shut the door, my watch says 9.26;
I walk down those few stairs again, determined, above all, to
    pass time.

ii

Having spent all my life not merely in one city,
But in a tightly circumscribed part of one city,
I find that most of the significant doors in my life
Opened and shut within a few minutes of each other.

iii

A leisurely evening walk could unite the four of them;
Have I really never gone on such a walk before?
It is autumn, and again the sky is completely dark;
It is the wrong time of the evening to have crowds on the
    streets.

ANGUS MARTIN (b. 1952)

Forest

For Sid Gallagher

Since I lately came to live
in an old house with a fire in it,
wood has got into my vision.

I put my saw to wood
and glance a nick, and then I cut
wood into bits that please me.

Weight and form may please me,
and I am pleased to own
what at last I have to burn.

I am a Scottish wood-collector;
I belong to a great tradition
of bleeding hands and thick coats.

Wood accumulates about me;
I build it into piles,
I bag it and I lug it.

I love the look of wood:
its surfaces are maps and pictures,
and staring eyes and voiceless mouths.

Wood to the end is unresisting:
it lets me lift and drag it
far from that place that it lay down.

Wood will never fight
the blade's truncating stroke
or scream when fire consumes it.

But I had dreams of wood.
I was alone in a high forest,
sun and seasons banished.

The trees bent down their silent heads
and closed their branches round about
and I was gathered into air.

I burn in my dreams of wood,
a melting torch suspended
in the dark heart of a silent forest.

JOHN GLENDAY (b. 1952)

The Apple Ghost

A musty smell of dampness filled the room
Where wrinkled green and yellow apples lay
On folded pages from an August newspaper.

She said:
'My husband brought them in, you understand,
Only a week or two before he died.
He never had much truck with waste, and
I can't bring myself to throw them out.
He passed away so soon . . .'

I understood then how the wonky kitchen door,
And the old Austin, settling upon its
Softened tyres in the wooden shed,
Were paying homage to the absence of his quiet hands.

In the late afternoon, I opened
Shallow cupboards where the sunlight leaned on
Shelf over shelf of apples, weightless with decay.
Beneath them, sheets of faded wallpaper
Showed ponies prancing through a summer field.
This must have been the only daughter's room
Before she left for good.

I did not sleep well.

The old woman told me over breakfast
How the boards were sprung in that upper hall;
But I knew I had heard his footsteps in the night,
As he dragged his wasted body to the attic room
Where the angles of the roof slide through the walls,
And the fruit lay blighted by his helpless gaze.

I knew besides that, had I crossed to the window
On the rug of moonlight,
I would have seen him down in the frosted garden,
Trying to hang the fruit back on the tree.

DILYS ROSE (b. 1954)

Fetish

Whisper if you must
But the walls absorb all confession
  – I've run through this ritual so often
  If he insists, I make a confession
  Kid on his demand has me truly enthralled
  If that's not sufficient try *deeply appalled.*

Your wish, for the moment, is my command
I'm mistress of every disguise
Is it rubber fur leather or silk I've to use
To pull the wool over your eyes?
Watch me concoct your burning obsession
Spell out your lust, own up to your passion.

So that's all it was that you wanted
A secret so paltry – I'd never have guessed
It could send a man scouring the town.
A scrap of mock silk – I'm no longer impressed.
You looked like the type who'd know I don't tout
My quality goods. See yourself out.

ROBIN ROBERTSON (b. 1955)

Fugue for Phantoms

This is the heart's thorn: the red rinse of memory;
this is the call of the coronach – keening, keening
over the water, haunted water,
the pitched grey, gull-swept sea.

This is the net and trident, thrown and retrieved,
thrown again; this is the death we live through –
our own thoughts are the mesh that's cast,
that let in the past with a stabbing spear.

These are the strange stigmata, the memories that bleed;
these are the luminous ghosts: lures
on the barb that pulls the heart from darkness
and silence, to the surface of the sea.

Where they have risen, the sea-dead, bobbing in effigy:
skin gone to curd, and worn now like a fragile dress,
water behind the eyes like the insides of oyster shells;
their huge heads puckered, their faces pursed like lips.

I would commit it all to the deep;
I want never to remember anything of this.

JOHN BURNSIDE (b. 1955)

The Blind

On Tuesdays they walked from the school
to the public baths,

passing our window, leaving us unseen
in every weather: flecked with snow or rain,

they marched in pairs, a good eight hundred yards
of guesswork.

All afternoon I pictured them
swimming in silence,

attuned to one another through the play
of water and skin,

imagining some kinship with the drowned
they might possess, unknowing: how they would guess

at motion and other lives
through the palm-smooth tiles;

and later, through trig,
I heard them walking back

and waited for the first blithe face to show
beyond the fence, the tap of whited canes

tracing a current home, through bricks and tar:
magnetic; guided; rooting in the darkness.

Out of Exile

When we are driving through the border towns
we talk of houses, empty after years
of tea and conversation;
of afternoons marooned against a clock
and silences elected out of fear,
of lives endured for what we disbelieved.

We recognise the shop fronts and the names,
the rushing trees and streets into the dark;
we recognise a pattern in the sky:
blackness flapping like a broken tent,
shadow foxes running in the stars,
But what we recognise is what we bring.

Driving, early, through the border towns,
the dark stone houses clanging at our wheels,
and we invent things as they might have been:
a light switched on, some night, against the cold,
and children at the door, with bags and coats,
telling stories, laughing, coming home.

CAROL ANN DUFFY (b. 1955)

Plainsong

Stop. Along this path, in phrases of light,
trees sing their leaves. No Midas touch
has turned the wood to gold, late in the year
when you pass by, suddenly sad, straining
to remember something you're sure you knew.

Listening. The words you have for things die
in your heart, but grasses are plainsong,
patiently chanting the circles you cannot repeat
or understand. This is your homeland,
Lost One, Stranger who speaks with tears.

It is almost impossible to be here and yet
you kneel, no one's child, absolved by late sun
through the branches of a wood, distantly
the evening bell reminding you, *Home, Home,
Home*, and the stone in your palm telling the time.

Pilate's Wife

Firstly, his hands – a woman's. Softer than mine,
with pearly nails, like shells from Galilee.
Indolent hands. Camp hands that clapped for grapes.
Their pale, mothy touch made me flinch. Pontius.

I longed for Rome, home, someone else. When the Nazarene
entered Jerusalem, my maid and I crept out,
bored stiff, disguised, and joined the frenzied crowd.
I tripped, clutched the bridle of an ass, looked up

and there he was. His face? Ugly. Talented.
He looked at me. I mean he looked at *me*. My God.
His eyes were eyes to die for. Then he was gone,
his rough men shouldering a pathway to the gates.

The night before his trial, I dreamt of him.
His brown hands touched me. Then it hurt.
Then blood. I saw that each tough palm was skewered
by a nail. I woke up, sweating, sexual, terrified.

Leave him alone. I sent a warning note, then quickly dressed.
When I arrived, the Nazarene was crowned with thorns.
The crowd was baying for Barabbas. Pilate saw me,
looked away, then carefully turned up his sleeves

and slowly washed his useless, perfumed hands.
They seized the prophet then and dragged him out,
up to the Place of Skulls. My maid knows all the rest.
Was he God? Of course not. Pilate believed he was.

MICK IMLAH (b. 1956)

Goldilocks

This is a story about the possession of beds.
It begins at the foot of a staircase in Oxford, one midnight,
When (since my flat in the suburbs of London entailed
A fiancée whose claims I did not have the nerve to evict)

I found myself grateful for climbing alone on a spiral
To sleep I could call with assurance exclusively mine,
For there was the name on the oak that the Lodge had
     assigned
Till the morning to me (how everything tends to its place!)

And flushed with the pleasing (if not unexpected) success
Of the paper on 'Systems of Adult-to-Infant Regression'
With which the Young Fireball had earlier baffled his betters
At the Annual Excuse for Genetics to let down its ringlets,

I'd just sniggered slightly (pushing the unlocked door
Of the room where I thought there was nothing of mine to
     protect)
To observe that my theory, so impudent in its address
To the Masters of Foetal Design and their perfect disciples,

Was rubbish – and leant to unfasten the window a notch,
When I suddenly grasped with aversion before I could see it
The fact that the bed in the corner directly behind me
Had somebody in it. A little ginger chap,

Of the sort anthropologists group in the genus of *tramp*,
Was swaddled, as though with an eye to the state of the
     sheets,
With half of his horrible self in the pouch of the bedspread
And half (both his raggled and poisonous trouser-legs) out;

Whose snore, like the rattle of bronchial stones in a bucket,
Resounded the length and the depth and the breadth of the
    problem
Of how to establish in safety a climate conducive
To kicking him out – till at last I could suffer no longer

The sight of his bundle of curls on my pillow, the proof
That even the worst of us look in our sleep like the angels
Except for a few. I closed to within a yard
And woke him, with a curt hurrahing sound.

And he reared in horror, like somebody late for work
Or a debutante subtly apprised of a welcome outstayed,
To demand (not of me, but more of the dreary familiar
Who exercised in its different styles the world's

Habit of persecution, and prodded him now)
Phit time is it? – so you'd think that it made any difference –
So you'd think after all that the berth had a rota attached
And Ginger was wise to some cynical act of encroachment;

But when, with a plausible echo of fatherly firmness,
I answered, 'It's bedtime' – he popped out and stood in a
    shiver,
And the released smell of his timid existence swirled
Like bracing coffee between our dissimilar stances.

Was there a dim recollection of tenement stairways
And jam and the Rangers possessed him, and sounded a
    moment
In creaks of remorse? 'Ah'm sorry, son – Ah couldnae tell
They'd hae a wee boy sleepin here – ye know?'

(And I saw what a file of degradations queued
In his brown past, to explain how Jocky there
Could make me out to be innocent and wee:
As if to be wee was not to be dying of drink;

As if to be innocent meant that you still belonged
Where beds were made for one in particular.)
Still, the lifespan of sociable feelings is shortest of all
In the breast of the migrant Clydesider; and soon he relapsed

Into patterns of favourite self-pitying sentiments. 'Son –
Ah'm warse than – Ah cannae, ye know? Ah'm off tae ma
     dandy!
Ah've done a wee josie – aye, wheesh! – it's warse what Ah'm
     gettin –
Aye – warse!' And again the appeal to heredity – 'Son.'

(In the course of his speech, the impostor had gradually
     settled
Back on the bed, and extended as visual aids
His knocked-about knuckles; tattooed with indelible foresight
On one set of these was the purple imperative SAVE.)

Now I'm keen for us all to be just as much worse as we want,
In our own time and space – but not, after midnight, in my
     bed;
And to keep his inertia at bay, I went for the parasite,
Scuttling him off with a shout and the push of a boot

That reminded his ribs I suppose of a Maryhill barman's,
Until I had driven him out of the door and his cough
Could be heard to deteriorate under a clock in the landing.
(Och, if he'd known *I* was Scottish! Then I'd have got it.)

     *

But of course he came back in the night, when I
                         dreamed I was coughing
And he stood by the door in the composite guise of a
     woman –
A mother, a doting landlady, a shadowy wife –
Sleepless as always, relieved nonetheless to have found me,

Or half-relieved – given what I had become;
Saying – 'It's just from the coughing and so on I wondered
If maybe a tramp had got into your bedroom' – and then,
Disappointedly: 'Couldn't you spare a wee thought for your
   dad?'

(I thought I was dreaming again on the train in the morning
To hear at my shoulder, before I had properly settled,
'Excuse me – is this seat taken?' spastically spoken;
But it wasn't our friend that I humoured through Didcot,
   and Reading,

No, but an anoracked spotter of diesels from Sheffield
Whose mind was apparently out in the sidings at Crewe:
Only one more in a world of unwanted connexions,
Who waved like a child when I fled for the toilet at Ealing.)

   *

This is my gloss on the story of Goldilocks. Note:
It uncovers a naked and difficult thought about beds,
Namely, that seldom again will there ever be one
With only you in it; take that however you will.

ELIZABETH BURNS (b. 1957)

The Oddity

She is a crooked planet: does not fit
in the thin universe of this house
that peoples itself with gentlefolk
who blink as though they do not see her
when she asks to use the library.

There is a clanking housekeeper
whose spiked mouth, licked, would give off poison,
and a cluster of maidservants
who, in the mothballed linen cupboard,
will gossip on the newcomer.

It's whispered that she's delicate
is delivered of bowls of sopped bread
bland milk puddings
but Cook sees her, the little witch,
sneaking herbs from the kitchen garden.

This household's under the thumb
of the chimes of the grandfather clock
Nothing here is tainted by imagination's kiss
and nothing queer-eyed or peculiarly skinned
gets out to roam the corridors

so that she, with her silences and pencils
her barefoot tiptoeing over the flagstones
in her old grey muslin dress
that billows out in draughty stairwells
feels freak: hears laughter

frothing in the steamy kitchen
whispers bubbling under doors,
is trailed by soft footsteps, rustling silks,
but reaches the room: a fastness:
turns the brass key in the lock behind her.

Soon there will be apron-smothered giggles
outside her door: she will rise
stuff the keyhole with a handkerchief
to block the peering eyes
then draw the shades against the lilac sky

and in thin dusk-light; take ink,
begin, in copperplate,
though hot tears plop, and blot the page,
and voices batter at her head
like scatty moths, to write.

ROBERT CRAWFORD (b. 1959)

Scotland in the 1890s

'I came across these facts which, mixed with others ...'
Thinking of Helensburgh, J. G. Frazer
Revises flayings and human sacrifice;
Abo of the Celtic Twilight, St Andrew Lang
Posts him a ten-page note on totemism
And a coloured fairy book – an Oxford man
From Selkirk, he translates Homer in his sleep.

'When you've lived here, even for a short time,
Samoa's a bit like Scotland – there's the sea ...
Back in Auld Reekie with a pen that sputtered
I wrote my ballad, "Ticonderoga" or
"A Legend of the West Highlands", then returned
To King Kalakaua's beach and torches –
You know my grandfather lit Lismore's south end?'

Mr Carnegie has bought Skibo Castle.
His Union Jack's sewn to the stars and stripes.
James Murray combs the dialect from his beard
And files slips for his massive *Dictionary*.
Closing a fine biography of mother,
Remembering Dumfries, and liking boys,
James Barrie, caught in pregnant London silence,
Begins to conceive the Never Never Land.

Knowledge

Ferrier invents the word *epistemology*
Sitting in a doorway wiped across with light

From an early flashgun. Round him, young buck students
Scatter in the aftershock, vanish.

*

Euclidean rain stots on cobbles
In wintry St Andrews. Ferrier hunches with cold,

Drawing his black gown over his head
Like a photographer, abolishing himself.

*

A sore has developed, a gland gone syphilitic.
He reads up the chemistry of mercuric oxide,

Hears his Aunt Susan, the famour author
Of *Marriage*, has died in her sleep.

*

Frail, he blocks a lecture-room entrance.
A New Woman confronts him: 'I wish to know

By what right you keep me from these Chemistry lectures.'
He can't move, at one with the stone.

IAIN BAMFORTH (b. 1959)

Men on Fire

Being a land of dissent and magnificent defeats
it evolved a subtle theology of failure, stealing its own
    thunder
wherever two or three were gathered together
and the occult plumbing groaned querulously beneath the
    boards.

These days, it grows owlish with hindsight –
recounting itself as a salvo of rain far north on mappamundi,
who's who of a supernumerary Creation myth
that swallowed the serpent's tail, ate the offspring whole.

When Rousseau exhumed the weather over Waverley
its civil imaginary became a fast diminishing return.
Few Encyclopaedists recall the genealogy backpacked out of
    Troy
or the vernacular of a silver-tongued Golden Age.

Later it saw itself arsy-versy, a nation after the letter;
but common cause outreaching the Dutch
it sold its birthright for a cut of the glory ...
a mere idea, it seemed invincible.

Yet it thrived on its own lost cause, and the mark of Cain
was a lefthandedness it practised righteously –
its sentinel cities on the plain a gritty paradigm
for an industry of calloused hands.

Guilt was one thing it exported to the new world;
ballast to the quantum energy ascending through midnight
    suns
as a monument of candour, men on fire:
here, in the old, sorrow recurs as a brief downpour,

dream-fug, supplements to a Journal of the Plague Year
when the gospel of virtues, that manic uprightness,
laid blame at nobody's door but its own . . .
beyond reach of heaven was a legislature pining for hell.

Out of it, sons and daughters have no clear sighting
of how an apple-tree opens the debate
but know it does, since they find themselves
on a mission without a motor, reciting the plot backwards

while pavements become rain-sleeked and lustral
and an oddly buoyant cargo gospel
swims through anti-matter to the hard edge of the landscape.
Like a native technology, it starts from what's left

and salvages its own future, a startled Doric narrative
stalking the wet track, tongue and tinder
to its radical children, shy to touch the incontrovertible ores
of a faith that has lately outgrown its disappointment.

DAVID KINLOCH (b. 1959)

The Voyage
for Donny O'Rourke

Baudelaire's mother sent him to sea
To cure him of the vice of verse.

But at Saint-Denis de Bourbon
He tried to disembark

Through rough waves to a sea-saw
Jetty with selected Balzac

Tucked beneath his arm.

Through twelve feet of ocean
The poet climbed the small boat's

Ladder but in the elevator
Of Mauritian water

Found himself alone at last
With the Human Comedy,

Swept up in its mane of emerald eyes,
Heard poems swimming striped

And suddenly yellow in his brain,
Then stepped like Aphrodite

Up to dry land, books fast
But opening in his hands.

DONNY O'ROURKE (b. 1959)

Clockwork

Broken clocks and watches were my father's hobby,
Killing time, he'd say, no irony intended, –
So grandfathers loitered dumbstruck in our lobby,
Hands salaaming as if begging to be mended.

Testimonial tokens of lifetimes on the job
Added to his pile their grateful mollusc gape.
Stammering snuff-stain waistcoat fob –
Tick corrected by puff and scrape.

Eyeglass squinched, he'd read the auguries,
Pronounce and whistle, arrange his tiny tools,
Wind the watch until we'd hear it wheeze,
Teaching me to prod among the cogs and spools

Though my cack-handedness loomed larger through his
    glass
He didn't mind the knack not passing on
It's a stoic's pastime, letting time pass,
He knew with quartz and plastic his day had gone

Now Dad's hands are slow and he's lost his spring
His face is scuffed by the emery-paper years
But he can value a clock by its pendulum swing
Or a watch, by the tact, of the tick, that he hears

And on Sundays sometimes we still repair
To smile at every bang on mantel chime
So many hunched gloamings unwinding there
My father and I keeping perfect time.

Praise of a Crofter

You'd shove, unknocking, into the croft on the hill where I
    sat in easy despairing
Over the page's bounded snow, and mutter about the rain-
    soaked hay,
The tatties you brought in your bucket, and how the beasts
    were faring –
Storm-unignorable, sweeping my bland blue heaven of
    choices away

With the one word, *Now*. Old drunkard, stubbly abstraction-
    hater, washer 'Wunce a week',
When you'd strip to a vest that hung there in rags as if you
    were freshly tiger-mauled,
Mocker, your laughter bright as the skies, of the folly of what
    I sought, or seek;
Jim Harcus, Jim Harcus, if forever's a lifetime, the name you
    are forever called,

When I went to the North expecting to praise elementals and
    skies,
There you awaited, wheezing like a steam-train, blunt as a
    hail shower –
And more remarkable soon your gale-blazed cheeks and
    ship-containing blue of your eyes
Than argosies dreamt on the seas in a golden hour;

Exemplar of the actual, of the sense I'd have in my every line,
You, clang-solid, brine-bitter, standing over the West's
Atlantic, clouds arranged about your head,
Or hunching, tractor-borne, through showers, to mend a
fence to keep in your beasts with twine,
No sipper at bottles, drinker at the fresh original spring of the
unread,

Dreader of the kirkyard's harbour, you hoarded in boxes and
letters a life, served up dire home-brew;
Island Apemantus, godless religious man, digger of friends'
deep graves,
Funeral attender out in unboundaried air on your tractor,
beside the expansive blue
Drowning the sight of the eye, the final resolving brine that
dooms and saves,

Thank you, for the many a dark-encircled night we sat up
late;
No case of liking you or not: simply there, in your wire-twist-
buttoned coat;
Reliable as tatties in your bucket, and strong as an iron gate;
Perching the bird of the real in my mind – and anchor, for
the spirit's boat.

W. N. HERBERT (b. 1961)

The Black Wet*

It's raining stair-rods and chairlegs,
it's raining candelabra and microwaves,
it's raining eyesockets.
When the sun shines through the shower
it's raining the hair of Sif,
each strand of which is real gold
(carat unknown).

It's raining jellyfish,
it's raining nuts, bolts and pineal glands,
it's raining a legion of fly noyades,
it's raining marsupials and echnidae,
it's raining anoraks in profusion.
It's siling, it's spittering, it's stotting, it's teeming,
it's pouring, it's snoring, it's plaining, it's Spaining.

People look up, open their mouths momentarily,
and drown.
People look out of windows and say,
'Send it down, David.'
Australians remark, 'Huey's missing the bowl.'
Americans reply, 'Huey, Dewie and Louie
are missing the bowl.'

It's not merely raining,
it's Windering and Thirling, it's Buttering down.
It's raining lakes, it's raining grass-snakes,
it's raining Bala, Baikal, and balalaikas,
it's raining soggy sidewinders and sadder adders.
It's raining flu bugs, Toby jugs and hearth-rugs,
it's raining vanity.

The sky is one vast water-clock
and it's raining seconds, it's raining years:
already you have spent more of your life looking at the rain
than you have sleeping, cooking, shopping and making love.
It's raining fusilli and capeletti,
it's raining mariners and albatrosses,
it's raining iambic pentameters.

Let's take a rain-check:
it's raining houndstooth and pinstripe,
it's raining tweed. This is the tartan of McRain.
This is the best test of the wettest west:
it is not raining locusts – just.
Why rain pests
when you can rain driving tests?

It is raining through the holes in God's string vest.

* *The black wet* (Scots): rain as opposed to snow.

130

JACKIE KAY (b. 1961)

Dance of the Cherry Blossom

Both of us are getting worse
Neither knows who had it first

He thinks I gave it to him
I think he gave it to me

Nights chasing clues where
One memory runs into another like dye.

Both of us are getting worse
I know I'm wasting precious time

But who did he meet between
May 87 and March 89.

I feel his breath on my back
A slow climb into himself then out.

In the morning it all seems different
Neither knows who had it first

We eat breakfast together – newspapers
And silence except for the slow slurp of tea

This companionship is better than anything
He thinks I gave it to him.

By lunchtime we're fighting over some petty thing
He tells me I've lost my sense of humour

I tell him I'm not Glaswegian
You all think death is a joke

It's not funny. I'm dying for fuck's sake
I think he gave it to me.

Just think he says it's every couple's dream
I won't have to wait for you up there

I'll have you night after night – your glorious legs
Your strong hard belly, your kissable cheeks

I cry when he says things like that
My shoulders cave in, my breathing trapped

Do you think you have a corner on dying
You self-pitying wretch, pathetic queen.

He pushes me; we roll on the floor like whirlwind;
When we are done in, our lips find each other

We touch soft as breeze, caress the small parts
Rocking back and forth, his arms become mine

There's nothing outside but the noise of the wind
The cherry blossom's dance through the night.

KATHLEEN JAMIE (b. 1962)

The Way We Live

Pass the tambourine, let me bash out praises
to the Lord God of movement, to Absolute
non-friction, flight, and the scary side:
death by avalanche, birth by failed contraception.
Of chicken tandoori and reggae, loud, from tenements,
commitment, driving fast and unswerving
friendship. Of tee-shirts on pulleys, giros and Bombay,
barmen, dreaming waitresses with many fake-gold
bangles. Of airports, impulse, and waking to uncertainty,
to strip-lights, motorways, or that pantheon –
the mountains. To overdrafts and grafting

and the fit slow pulse of wipers as you're
creeping over Rannoch, while the God of moorland
walks abroad with his entourage of freezing fog,
his bodyguard of snow.
Of endless gloaming in the North, of Asiatic swelter,
to launderettes, anecdotes, passions and exhaustion,
Final Demands and dead men, the skeletal grip
of government. To misery and elation; mixed,
the sod and caprice of landlords.
To the way it fits, the way it is, the way it seems
to be: let me bash out praises – pass the tambourine.

Arraheids

See thon raws o flint arraheids
in oor gret museums o antiquities
awful grand in Embro –
Dae'ye near'n daur wunner at wur histrie?
Weel then, Bewaur!

The museums of Scotland are wrang.
They urnae arraheids
but a show o grannies' tongues,
the hard tongues o grannies
aa deid an gaun
back to thur peat and burns,
but for thur sherp
chert tongues, that lee
fur generations in the land
like wicked cherms, that lee
aa douce in the glessy cases in the gloom
o oor museums, an
they arnae lettin oan. But if you daur
sorn aboot an fancy
the vanished hunter, the wise deer runnin on;
wheesht . . . an you'll hear them,
fur they cannae keep fae muttering
ye arnae here tae wonder,
whae dae ye think ye ur?

Nil Nil

*Just as any truly accurate representation of a particular geography
can only exist on a scale of 1:1 (imagine the vast, rustling map of
Burgundy, say, settling over it like a freshly starched sheet!) so it is
with all our abandoned histories, those ignoble lines of succession
that end in neither triumph nor disaster, but merely plunge on into
deeper and deeper obscurity; only in the infinite ghost-libraries of
the imagination – their only possible analogue – can their ends be
pursued, the dull and terrible facts finally authenticated.*

François Aussemain, *Pensées*

From the top, then, the zenith, the silent footage:
McGrandle, majestic in ankle-length shorts,
his golden hair shorn to an open book, sprinting
the length of the park for the long hoick forward,
his balletic toe-poke nearly bursting the roof
of the net; a shaky pan to the Erskine St End
where a plague of grey bonnets falls out of the clouds.
But ours is a game of two halves, and this game
the semi they went on to lose; from here
it's all down, from the First to the foot of the Second,
McGrandle, Visocchi and Spankie detaching
like bubbles to speed the descent into pitch-sharing,
pay-cuts, pawned silver, the Highland Division,
the absolute sitters ballooned over open goals,
the dismal nutmegs, the scores so obscene
no respectable journal will print them; though one day
Farquhar's spectacular bicycle-kick
will earn him a name-check in Monday's obituaries.
Besides the one setback – the spell of giant-killing
in the Cup (Lochee Violet, then Aberdeen Bon Accord,
the deadlock with Lochee Harp finally broken
by Farquhar's own-goal in the replay)

nothing inhibits the fifty-year slide
into Sunday League, big tartan flasks,
open hatchbacks parked squint behind goal-nets,
the half-time satsuma, the dog on the pitch,
then the Boy's Club, sponsored by Skelly Assurance,
then Skelly Dry Cleaners, then nobody;
stud-harrowed pitches with one-in-five inclines,
grim fathers and perverts with Old English Sheepdogs
lining the touch, moaning softly.
Now the unrefereed thirty-a-sides,
terrified fat boys with calipers minding
four jackets on infinite, notional fields;
ten years of dwindling, half-hearted kickabouts
leaves two little boys – Alastair Watt,
who answers to 'Forty', and wee Horace Madden,
so smelly the air seems to quiver above him –
playing desperate two-touch with a bald tennis ball
in the hour before lighting-up time.
Alastair cheats, and goes off with the ball
leaving wee Horace to hack up a stone
and dribble it home in the rain;
past the stopped swings, the dead shanty-town
of allotments, the black shell of Skelly Dry Cleaners
and into his cul-de-sac, where, accidentally,
he neatly back-heels it straight into the gutter
then tries to swank off like he meant it.

Unknown to him, it is all that remains
of a lone fighter-pilot, who, returning at dawn
to find Leuchars was not where he'd left it,
took time out to watch the Sidlaws unsheathed
from their great black tarpaulin, the haar burn off Tayport
and Venus melt into Carnoustie, igniting
the shoreline; no wind, not a cloud in the sky
and no one around to admire the discretion
of his unscheduled exit: the engine plopped out

and would not re-engage, sending him silently
twirling away like an ash-key,
his attempt to bail out only partly successful,
yesterday having been April the 1st –
the ripcord unleashing a flurry of socks
like a sackful of doves rendered up to the heavens
in private irenicon. He caught up with the plane
on the ground, just at the instant the tank blew
and made nothing of him, save for his fillings,
his tackets, his lucky half-crown and his gallstone,
now anchored between the steel bars of a stank
that looks to be biting the bullet on this one.

In short, this is where you get off, reader;
I'll continue alone, on foot, in the failing light,
following the trail as it steadily fades
into road-repairs, birdsong, the weather, nirvana,
the plot thinning down to a point so refined
not even the angels could dance on it. Goodbye.

00:00: Law Tunnel

(leased to the Scottish Mushroom Company after its closure in 1927)

(i)

In the airy lull
between the wars
they cut the rails
and closed the doors

on the stalled freight:
crate on crate
of blood and earth –
the shallow berth

of the innocents,
their long room
stale and tense
with the same dream

(ii)

Strewn among
the ragged queue –
the snoring king
and his retinue,

Fenrir, Pol Pot,
Captain Oates
and the leprechauns –
are the teeth, the bones

and begging-cup
of the drunken piper.
The rats boiled up
below the sleepers

(iii)

The crippled boy
of Hamelin
pounds away
at the locked mountain

waist-deep in thorn
and all forlorn,
he tries to force
the buried doors

I will go to my mother
and sing of my shame
I will grow up to father
the race of the lame

ANGELA MCSEVENEY (b. 1964)

The Lump

Rolling over in a hot June night
I cradled my breasts in my arms
and felt a hard knot of tissue.

I was fifteen.
My life rose up in my throat
and threatened to stifle me.

It took three attempts to tell my mother.
She promised that my appointment would be
with a woman doctor.

A nurse called my name.
I didn't have cancer.

The stitches in my skin reminded me
of a chicken trussed for the oven.

I felt ashamed
that the first man to see me
had only been doing his job.

The Winter Rose
for Dr James Hawkins

Blue-handed, with difficult string,
I staked the broken winter rose,

unbending fibres of green spine,
lifting a crumpled white face –

rain-teared, blinded with earth;
finished by axing winds.

So many thorns hid in the leaves,
and light so thin,

my task lasted even as snow
rehearsed Christmas in the garden.

And when I would have drowned
in snow, an angel came –
I had no words or gold.

But I saw the crushed bush
ghosted with buds;

her face now upturned – furred,
snug in snow – to stars;

after sleeping summer
ironing new petals with air.

And when I would have drowned
in snow, an angel came –
I had no words or gold.

KATE CLANCHY (b. 1965)

Poem for a Man with No Sense of Smell

This is simply to inform you:

that the thickest line in the kink of my hand
smells like the feel of an old school desk,
the deep carved names worn sleek with sweat;

that beneath the spray of my expensive scent
my armpits sound a bass note strong
as the boom of a palm on a kettle drum;

that the wet flush of my fear is sharp
as the taste of an iron pipe, midwinter,
on a child's hot tongue; and that sometimes,

in a breeze, the delicate hairs on the nape
of my neck, just where you might bend
your head, might hesitate and brush your lips,

hold a scent frail and precise as a fleet
of tiny origami ships, just setting out to sea.

RODDY LUMSDEN (b. 1966)

Yeah Yeah Yeah

No matter what you did to her, she said,
There's times, she said, she misses you, your face
Will pucker in her dream, and times the bed's
Too big. Stray hairs will surface in a place
You used to leave your shoes. A certain phrase,
Some old song on the radio, a joke
You had to be there for, she said, some days
It really gets to her; the way you smoked
Or held a cup, or her, and how you woke
Up crying in the night sometimes, the way
She'd stroke and hush you back, and how you broke
Her still. All this she told me yesterday,
Then she rolled over, laughed, began to do
To me what she so rarely did with you.

TRACEY HERD (b. 1968)

Coronach

The skylark's melody is sealed in ice:
a coronach as blue as the winter
sky. The moon wobbles over the rock face,
throwing into high relief the climber
in a gully below the glittering maze.

He is a brilliant figure in this frieze.
His genius walked him into space
and left him to find a foothold there.
The moon is sheer ice or a cracked watch-face
that swings on its fragile chain of stars.

Night is falling at its own modest pace.

ACKNOWLEDGEMENTS

For permission to reprint copyright material the publishers gratefully acknowledge the following:

IAN ABBOT: 'A Body of Work' from *Avoiding the Gods* (Chapman, 1988) by permission of Chapman. MARION ANGUS: 'Alas! Poor Queen' from *Selected Poems* (Serif Books, 1950) by permission of Faber and Faber Limited. IAIN BAMFORTH: 'Men on Fire' from *Sons and Pioneers* (Carcanet, 1992) by permission of Carcanet Press Ltd. D.M. BLACK: 'Kew Gardens' from *Collected Poems 1964–87* (Polygon, 1991) by permission of Polygon. ALAN BOLD: 'A Special Theory of Relativity' by permission of the late Alan Bold. GEORGE MACKAY BROWN: 'Old Fisherman with Guitar', 'Trout Fisher' and 'Kirkyard' from *Selected Poems 1954–1983* (John Murray, 1991) by permission of John Murray (Publishers) Ltd. ELIZABETH BURNS: 'The Oddity' from *Ophelia and Other Poems* (Polygon, 1991) by permission of Polygon. JOHN BURNSIDE: 'Out of Exile' from *The Hoop* (Carcanet Press, 1988) by permission of Carcanet Press Limited; 'The Blind', from *A Normal Skin* (Jonathan Cape, 1997) by permission of Random House UK. RON BUTLIN: 'This Evening' from *Ragtime in Unfamiliar Bars* (Secker & Warburg, 1985) © Ron Butlin, 1985, by permission of Martin Secker and Warburg Limited. GERRY CAMBRIDGE: 'Praise of a Crofter' from *The Shell House* (Scottish Cultural Press, 1995). NORMAN CAMERON: 'Green Green, is El Aghir' from *Collected Poems*, edited by W. Hope and J. Barker (Anvil Press, 1989) by permission of Anvil Press Poetry Ltd. KATE CLANCHY: 'Poem for a man with no sense of smell' from *Slattern* (Chatto & Windus, 1995). STEWART CONN: 'Todd' and 'On Craigie Hill' from *In the Kibble Palace: New and Selected Poems* (Bloodaxe Books, 1987) by permission of Bloodaxe Books Ltd. ROBERT CRAWFORD: 'Scotland in the 1890s' from *A Scottish Assembly* (Chatto & Windus, 1990) and 'Knowledge' from *Spirit Machines* (Jonathan Cape, 1999) by permission of Random Century Group. IVOR CUTLER: 'The Railway Sleepers' from *A Flat Man* (Trigram Press, 1977) by permission of the author. CAROL ANN DUFFY: 'Plainsong' from *Selling Manhattan* (Anvil Press, 1987), by permission of Anvil Press Poetry Ltd; and 'Pilate's Wife' from *The*

World's Wife (Picador, 1999) by permission. ALISON FELL: 'Pushing Forty' from *Kisses for Mayakovsky* (Virago Press, 1984) by permission of Peake Associates. GILLIAN FERGUSON: 'The Winter Rose' from *Air for Sleeping Fish* (Bloodaxe, 1997) by permission of Bloodaxe Books Ltd. ROBIN FULTON: 'Resolutions' from *Fields of Focus* (Anvil Press, 1982) by permission of Anvil Press Poetry Ltd. ROBERT GARIOCH: 'Glisk of the Great' and 'Heard in the Cougate' from *Complete Poetical Works* (Macdonald Publishers, 1983) by permission of The Saltire Society. VALERIE GILLIES: 'The Ericstane Brooch' from *The Chanter's Tune* (Canongate, 1990) by permission of Canongate Press Plc. JOHN GLENDAY: 'The Apple Ghost' from *The Apple Ghost* (Peterloo Poets, 1989) by permission of Peterloo Poets. W.S. GRAHAM: 'The Lying Dear' from *Collected Poems 1942–1977* (Faber, 1979) by permission of the Estate of W. S. Graham. ANDREW GREIG: 'In the Tool-shed' from *Surviving Passages* (Canongate, 1982) by permission of the author. GEORGE CAMPBELL HAY: 'Bisearta'/'Bizerta' from *Modern Scottish Gaelic Poems*, edited by D. Macaulay (Southside, 1976) by permission of Canongate Press Plc. HAMISH HENDERSON: 'Seven Good Germans' from *Elegies for the Dead in Cyrenaica* (Polygon, 1990) by permission of Polygon. W. N. HERBERT: 'The Black Wet' from *The Laurelude*. TRACEY HERD: 'Coronach' from *No Hiding Place* (Bloodaxe, 1998), by permission of Bloodaxe Books. MICK IMLAH: 'Goldilocks' from *Birthmarks* (Chatto & Windus, 1988) by permission of Random Century Group. KATHLEEN JAMIE: 'The Way We Live' from *The Way We Live* (Bloodaxe Books, 1987) and 'Arraheids' from *The Queen of Sheba* (Bloodaxe, 1994) by permission of Bloodaxe Books Ltd. JACKIE KAY; 'Dance of the Cherry Blossom' from *The Adoption Papers* (Bloodaxe Books, 1991) by permission of Bloodaxe Books Ltd. DAVID KINLOCH: 'The Voyage' from *Paris–Forfar* (Polygon, 1994). FRANK KUPPNER: 'Passing Through Doorways' from *The Intelligent Observation of Naked Women* (Carcanet Press, 1987) by permission of Carcanet Press Limited. TOM LEONARD: *from* 'Unrelated Incidents' and *from* 'Ghostie Men' from *Intimate Voices: Selected Work 1965–1983* (Galloping Dog Press, 1984) by permission of the author. LIZ LOCHHEAD: 'The Grim Sisters' and 'My Mother's Suitors' from *Dreaming Frankenstein and Collected Poems* (Polygon, 1984) by permission of Polygon. RODDY LUMSDEN: 'Yeah Yeah Yeah' from *Yeah, Yeah, Yeah* (Bloodaxe, 1997). GEORGE MACBETH:

SCOTT: 'The Mankind Toun' from *The Ship, and Ither Poems* (OUP, 1963) by permission of the late Tom Scott. BURNS SINGER: 'Peterhead in May' from *Selected Poems*, edited by A. Cluysenaar (Carcanet Press, 1977) by permission of Carcanet Press Limited. IAIN CRICHTON SMITH: 'The Law and the Grace', *from* 'The White Air of March' and 'Chinese Poem' from *Selected Poems* (Carcanet Press, 1985), 'Listen' from *The Village* (Carcanet Press, 1989) by permission of Carcanet Press Limited. SYDNEY GOODSIR SMITH: *from* 'Under the Eildon Tree – V: Slugabed' from *Collected Poems* (John Calder, 1975) Copyright © John Calder (Publishers) Ltd 1975, by permission of Calder Publications Ltd. WILLIAM SOUTAR: 'The Tryst' from *The Poems of William Soutar* edited by W. R. Aitken (Scottish Academic Press, 1988) by permission of The Trustees of The National Library of Scotland. MURIEL SPARK: 'Elegy in a Kensington Churchyard' from *Going Up to Sotheby's, and Other Poems* (Granada Publishing, 1982) by permission of David Higham Associates Limited. DERICK THOMSON: 'An Tobar'/'The Well', 'Srath Nabhair'/'Strathnaver' from *Creachadh na clarsaich . . . : Plundering the Harp. Collected Poems 1940–1980* (Macdonald Publishers, 1982) by permission of The Saltire Society. RUTHVEN TODD: 'Trout Flies' from *Garland for the Winter Solstice* (Dent, 1961) by permission of David Higham Associates Limited. SYDNEY TREMAYNE: 'A Burial' from *Selected and New Poems* (Chatto & Windus, 1973) Copyright © Sydney Tremayne, 1973, by permission of Sheil Land Associates Ltd. KENNETH WHITE: *from* 'Late August on the Coast' from *The Bird Path: Collected Longer Poems* (Mainstream Publishing, 1989) by permission of Mainstream Publishing Co. (Edinburgh) Ltd. ANDREW YOUNG: 'On the Pilgrim's Road' and 'The Shepherd's Hut' from *The Poetical Works* (Secker & Warburg, 1985) by permission of The Estate of Andrew Young. DOUGLAS YOUNG: 'For a Wife in Jizzen' from *A Clear Voice: Douglas Young, Poet and Polymath*, edited by C. Young and D. Murison (Macdonald Publishers, 1976) by permission of The Saltire Society.

Faber and Faber Limited apologize for any errors or omissions in the above list and would be grateful to be notified of any corrections that should be incorporated in the next edition or reprint of this volume.